M000034579

For Larry Caravella, a great guy and diehard Jets fan

TABLE OF CONTENTS

PROLOGUE: ONLY THE JETS... i

DOES ANYONE ELSE FEEL A DRAFT? 1
GAMETIME: LET THE PAIN BEGIN! 14
KILLER PLAYS 36
KILLER FANS 44
GANG GREEN FOR REAL 52
THIS IS NOT A CAROUSEL THAT YOU'D
WANT TO RIDE 60
NOT SO FREE AGENTS 74
THE OVER THE HILL GANG 80
WHO RUNS THIS TEAM, ANYWAY!?!? 88
STOP! THEY'RE ALREADY DEAD! 100
IT WASN'T ALWAYS THIS WAY... 108

EPILOGUE: BUT THAT WAS THEN, THIS IS NOW 112

Prologue

Only the Jets...

WHAT!?!?

NO SPIKE!?!?

WHAT IS GOING ON HERE!?!?

UGH! HERE WE GO AGAIN!

It's a cold, wet, afternoon on Sunday, November 27th, 1994. Any Jets fan knows what happened, and although they won't talk about it, they *will* tell you they wish it never *did* happen! OR: Any Jets fan knows what happened that day; but they will tell you that they wish it never *did* happen...OR: Any Jets fan remembers what happened; but they will tell you that they wish they could *forget* it happened...

On that fateful day, 75,606 fans filed into Giants Stadium (they didn't even have their own stadium!) in East Rutherford, New Jersey to see their beloved Jets take on their arch rival - the hated Miami Dolphins - led by the Jets' "supposed to be" franchise quarterback, Dan Marino, in week 12 of the 1994 season. Fans were STILL wondering, that day - HOW IN THE WORLD could we have passed on DAN MARINO - OF ALL PEOPLE! - WHEN HE PLOPPED INTO OUR (INCOMPETENT) LAP IN THE LATE 1ST ROUND OF THE 83 DRAFT!?!?!? It's ABSOLUTELY MIND BOGGLING!!

That Marino was accused of drug use - a charge for which there was no objective proof - had given the Jets brass pause. Thus, the Jets passed on him in favor of a guy who had set most of the NCAA passing records - IN DIVISION 2!!!!!!!

And speaking of divisions, the game this day pitted these two teams, joined by a common player but diverging stories, in a battle for the division lead of the AFC East. Both teams were tied for 1st place and looking to make that final playoff push, with the Jets trying to get back to the playoffs and once again make a run at the Super Bowl - their first Super Bowl since the heroic win under Joe Namath, he of the famous guarantee, in 1969 vs. the Baltimore Colts in what was, for Jets fans at least, "The Greatest Game Ever Played" and for others "The Game

J-E-T-S! Pain! Pain! PAIN!

That Forced the Merger" of the AFL with the NFL. The
Dolphins, on the other hand, were looking to get back to
the big game for the first time in a decade – in 1984, when
they were led by (who else?) Dan Marino, in only his
second year in the NFL. NBC recognized this importance,
reflected by assigning their main broadcast duo, Marv
Albert and Paul Maguire, to cover the game and
broadcasting it nationally.

Without a doubt, the biggest difference between the
two teams was at the Head Coaching position. The
Dolphins, enjoying yet another very successful season,
were led by the legendary Don Shula, one of the greatest
coaches of all time and already a multiple Super Bowl
champion. The Jets coach could not have been more
different - a young hotshot in his first year at the helm of
any team, who nonetheless seemed to have everything
going his way: Pete Carroll (who, of course, went on to
win a Super Bowl himself – but with Seattle, NOT THE
JETS!!).

The game starts and the Jets get off on the right foot,
building a 10-0 lead at the end of the 1st half. At this

point, Jets quarterback Boomer Esiason has had the better of the play and looks to be leading the Jets to a huge victory at home. By contrast, Dan Marino and the Dolphins are struggling to get anything going against a tough Jets defense. The 2nd half starts with a flurry of offensive activity as the teams trade touchdowns, scoring 2 apiece in the 3rd quarter. So heading into the 4th, the score now is Jets 24 Dolphins 14.

With just over 10 minutes to go in the game, Dan Marino finds his top receiver, Mark Ingram, for a 28-yard touchdown pass to cut the Jets lead to just 24-21. The teams trade several punts until, with only a little over 3 minutes left in the game, and the Jets clinging to a three point lead, Marino leads the Dolphins down the field, to the very doorstep of the end zone. Miami has two choices: attempt a game tying field goal and play for overtime; or go for a touchdown that would greatly help Miami clinch the game and the division lead.

Miami has the ball down at the Jets 8 yard line. With the clock at 25 seconds and ticking, Marino yells "CLOCK" three times to everyone, indicating that he will spike the ball, while moving his hand up and down in a spiking motion. The Jets, seeing this, expect him to spike it. Everyone in the stands expect him to spike it. The entire national audience - numbering in the millions - expect him to spike it... But -

HE DOESNT SPIKE IT!

WHAT!?!?

NO SPIKE!?!?

WHAT IS GOING ON HERE!?!?

Instead of spiking the ball, Marino takes a two step drop and finds Ingram on the right sideline, uncovered, in the endzone...

WHAT!?

WHAT!?!?

The only cheering you can hear is from the Dolphins' sideline. Miami's broadcast team of Bill Zimpfer and Jim Mandich are going crazy in the booth. But other than that, the whole stadium is dead silent and, as line judge Jeff Bergman would characterize it later, "everyone was shocked".

The play had actually come from former Browns

quarterback, now Dolphins backup, Bernie Kosar, who successfully ran the same play in 1986. Against...

Who else...?

The Jets fail to do anything with 3 minutes left. They have lost, blowing a 24-6 lead as well as losing the possibility for 1st place in the division. Jets players and coaches are dazed; the fans are shocked, everyone associated with the Jets can't fathom what just happened. Jets fans all over skulk home or to the local bar or wherever they go to drown their sorrows after yet another absolutely aggravating game which has become, by then, too often the norm.

On the way home from the game that day, Boomer Esiason helped a woman slumped over in her car as the result of an accident (mercifully, just a fender bender) near the Lincoln Tunnel. After he helped the lady, he was heckled by many Jets fans passing by. The Dolphins would end up going 10-6 and win the division. The Jets? They ended up losing the rest of their games that season, finishing with an abysmal 6-10 record...

An iconic moment - one that stands for ALL THE

J-E-T-S! Pain! Pain! PAIN!

PAIN that Jets fans have experienced over time, over all
the years, over all the decades of failure, frustration,
futility...

UGH! HERE WE GO AGAIN!

But wait -There's more!

Much more disappointment.

MUCH more irony.

MUCH MORE PAIN!

Only the Jets...

1

Does Anyone Else Feel A Draft?

Every late April, the NFL Draft takes center stage. It is supposed to be a time of optimism for all football fans to see their favorite franchise pick more talent to help it succeed. Who knows? Maybe they'll find the next Hall of Fame quarterback that will lead the team to the promised land. Or perhaps they'll draft a guy that becomes the missing piece they'll need to take it to the house - to go all the way; to win a Super Bowl. The possibilities are endless and everyone gets excited! BUT ...

If you are a Jets fan, the only excitement you'll ever get is to see what blunder of a pick the Jets will make each year - one that doesn't come EVEN CLOSE to panning out. There are no words to describe Jets drafting other than LEGENDARILY BAD!

It's the year 1981. The Jets are coming off an abysmal 4-12 campaign. They go into the draft with the third overall pick - the THIRD OVERALL PICK! And who do they select? Freeman McNeil, who would go on to become a solid halfback for the Jets, and fan favorite, for several seasons. YES baby! So far, so good. Alas, in the late second round, with Jets fans fully expecting the team to fill other holes, things turn, and not for the better. You might think that would be the obvious decision, right? Well then you certainly don't know the Jets!

Commissioner Pete Rozelle gets to the podium, Jets fans cheering with anticipation over who the Jets would take to bolster the team. And so, who do they wind up taking...? ANOTHER RUNNING BACK!

C'mon man, really?

Yes. With the 30th overall pick in the 2nd round, the New York Jets select... Marian Barber, out of the University of Minnesota. Barber, a running back, who was nothing more than a small blip on the radar. (If even that!) 74 carries for only 317 yards and 2 touchdowns...OVER 6 SEASONS!!!That's who!

Then we have the infamous 1983 Draft (PUBLIC SERVICE ANNOUNCEMENT: If you happen to be (you don't have to admit it out loud) a Jets fan, crawl under the covers, go back to sleep, and try to forget this one. The Jets had just lost in the AFC Championship game to the rival Miami Dolphins the previous year. The organization had made the decision that they needed a franchise QB, assessing starter Richard Todd's career pretty much at the end. The Jets needed to think about the future.

However, with the team holding the 24th selection, the Jets draft team expected that most of the top-rated QB's would be gone by then. However, one candidate in particular was still on the board. All of his college career the Jets had been interested in The University of Pittsburgh's Dan Marino (Remember him? Cf., the Prologue of this book). Marino, in his junior year, was projected to be the #1 overall pick in '82. Instead, he decided to stay in college for his senior season, but he threw twice as many interceptions than touchdowns in his final year. Understandably, this created considerable concern and eventually a problem for the Jets.

Marino had been accused of partying too much - even taking drugs such as cocaine. He voluntarily submitted to drug testing before every game of his senior season, each time showing that he was completely clean. However, many NFL scouts and general managers were not so sure. As a result, Marino's ranking continuously dropped in the 1st round. During that time, several other QBs were drafted (the list included not just Todd Blackledge and Tony Eason, but two future Hall of Famers, John Elway and Jim Kelly).

Once Jets fans saw Marino dropping, they began to

think it was pretty possible, even probable, that the Jets would pick Marino at 24. With every pick that went by, Jets fans got more and more excited.

Finally...pick #24 rolls around and Marino is still available! The fans are going nuts, high-fiving and celebrating before the pick even happens. NFL Commissioner Pete Rozelle walks up to the podium, the fans get louder and louder: We are going to draft Marino right? RIGHT!?

"With the 24th overall pick in the first round, The New York Jets select..."

Jets fans are blissful with anticipation...
"Quarterback..."

Yes, yes! Jets fans can already taste it! Marino! Marino!

"Ken O'Brien out of the University of California-Davis!"

Oh, somewhere in this favored land the sun is shining bright...

Pete Rozelle smiles and chuckles to himself after he announces the pick, leading Jets fans to see it as some kind of a perverse foreshadowing. Jets fans can't believe what has transpired - they all look around, shellshocked, asking the same question of one another...WHO IN THE

HOLY HELL IS KEN O'BRIEN!?!? That is the same question even Dan Marino asks himself when he hears the pick on TV in his home in Pittsburgh. And as if that isn't bad enough, a reporter goes up after the pick and mispronounces O'Brien's name - not once, not twice, but three times on live TV before he finally gets it right. Jets fans - at least those not catatonic from shock think: Only the Jets would do this; only Jets fans would have this happen to them.

O'Brien became a very good quarterback in his nine years with the Jets. He was the only QB in franchise history to lead the league in passing in a season - a feat even Joe Namath could not achieve. He even had a winning record against (you guessed it) Dan Marino in his career.

But, unfortunately, O'Brien could never quite get the Jets to that ever - elusive goal: The Lombardi Trophy. As for Marino? Well, he ended up being picked by the (brace yourself Jets fans) defending AFC Champion Miami Dolphins. He led Miami to the Super Bowl in just his second season and would go on to become one of the greatest quarterbacks in NFL history.

Oh, what might have been had the Jets taken Marino? Jets fans can only dream.

But, if you think that was bad, think again - it just gets worse and worse. Fast forward to 1989 and the Jets hold the 14th overall pick in the 1st round of the draft. A lot of Jets fans (still smarting) were expecting the Jets to look for some weapons to help out quarterback Ken O'Brien. There weren't many options in '89 so the Jets couldn't possibly screw this up, right? Right!?!?

WRONG! The Jets select Jeff Lageman, a defensive end from the University of Virginia. When the Jets announce their pick, Jets fans almost pass out! Lageman was an undersized defensive end who wasn't projected to be drafted until the late 1st/ early 2nd round. However, the Jets being the Jets, take him with the 14th overall selection. Lageman was serviceable in the NFL and played with the Jets from 89-94, but ONCE AGAIN they made a head-scratching decision.

And they continued in that tradition in 1992. The Jets held yet another top 15 pick and ONCE AGAIN, Jets fans were looking for a good pickup that could help solidify their offense. This time, they went after another unknown in Nebraska: Tight End Johnny Mitchell. AGAIN, Jets fans screamed in agony as their team continued the trend of surprising, and in their view, horrific draft selections. Mitchell had an almost ironic stint with the Jets. He

7

played his first three seasons with the team, compiling 16 catches for only 210 yards and 1 (count'em 1!!!) touchdown.

Then if that wasn't bad enough, in 1999, Mitchell begs then - Jets coach Bill Parcells to give him a chance to revive his career. Parcells does and all is good...for only a short time because only after the first day of training camp, HE GETS CUT! You can't make this stuff up!

Deja vu? Well, if you don't feel like you've seen this movie already before this point, you definitely will now! We move to the 1995 draft. The prize of this draft was one Warren Sapp - yes, THAT Warren Sapp - the University of Miami's All American defensive end and future Hall of Famer, Warren Sapp. Just like in 1983, the Jets felt they were unlikely to draft Sapp at #9 since he was projected to go #1 overall. However, JUST LIKE MARINO IN '83, Sapp, who was falsely accused of drug allegations began to drop. And, JUST LIKE IN '83, Jets fans were licking their chops in anticipation of the opportunity to draft the big bad #99 from the U. Well, pick #9 comes up and JUST LIKE IN '83, the big prize was there for the taking. As then-NFL commissioner Paul Tagliabue walked up to the podium you could hear the chanting of Jets fans shouting in unison, "WE WANT

SAPP, WE WANT SAPP, WE WANT SAPP"!

So you think the Jets would be wise to take Sapp here, right? RIGHT!?!? But no, you would have been a sap (sic) to think so...

Kyle Brady!?!? Who!?!?

Exactly! The Jets took tight end Kyle Brady out of Penn State and Sapp remained on the board. All Jets fans were understandably angry, shocked and confused. But wait - there's more! Also mind boggling is the fact that the Jets didn't even need Brady! They already had that position filled, but they took Brady anyway. Brady, of course, never became the player the Jets had hoped and was a journeyman for most of his career.

KYLE BRADY OVER WARREN SAPP??? SERIOUSLY!?!?

Yes, seriously.

Since we're on a roll (not unlike the Jets), how about when they got the #1 overall pick? Surely, they would get THIS right. You should know the rest, but in case you don't remember, I'll jog your memory...

It's the very next year - 1996 - and the Jets, after a 1-15 season, get the 1st overall pick. There were several great players available in this draft, including Jonathan Ogden, Ray Lewis (!!!!), Eddie George, and Simeon Rice. The

Jets take none of those guys and select talented wide receiver Keyshawn Johnson out of USC.

Now, Keyshawn was a solid wide receiver and he helped the Jets improve their record in his first two seasons in New York. However, his temperament was too much for the organization and they traded him to the Buccaneers for two 1st round picks. Keyshawn would go on to win the Super Bowl with the Bucs and became an even better player after his time with the Jets. He was definitely another one that got away.

The mid-2000's is when things REALLY got interesting. In 2008, the Jets held the 8th overall pick and one guy that many thought should have been a Jet was Delaware's Joe Flacco. That year however, was the year of Brett Favre and the carousel of him retiring and not retiring. The Jets felt they didn't need a QB (yeah right). So instead they draft one of the most talked about players in the draft in D-end, Vernon Gholston. Many believed that the Jets had hit the lottery and that their defense would become great. And sure enough it did, but Gholston was no part of it. In fact, he was let go by the Jets after 3 seasons finishing his time with the team with a whopping ZERO (as in none, bupkis, nada) SACKS! 0!!! Gholston became one of the biggest busts in NFL history.

The following year was 2009 (and Jets fans, you know where I'm going with this one). The Jets originally held the 14th pick and, with the failure of the infamous Brett Favre experiment and him fleeing to Minnesota, the Jets were in the market for a franchise QB. The prize was USC standout Mark Sanchez ("THE SANCHIZE!!!"). They were sure that he would be gone by the 14th pick though, so the Jets made a bold move and traded their 1st and 2nd round picks as well as three current players to the Cleveland Browns for the 5th overall pick. With that pick, the Jets... drafted MARK SANCHEZ! For once they hadn't messed it up! Sanchez would lead us to the promised land!

Wait - we're talking about the JETS here! Sanchez started his career on a roll, leading the Jets to back-to-back AFC Championships under then-head coach Rex, "Sexy Rexy", Ryan. Things were looking up so much that Ryan even got a tattoo of his wife...WEARING NOTHING BUT A MARK SANCHEZ JETS' JERSEY! It looked like the Jets had made the right choice.

But then it all fell apart somehow. Sanchez started to decline because SOMEBODY (The big man with the lap band?) was all about ground and pound, baby! Sanchez, a classic long ball thrower, didn't fit well into that scheme.

The team around him started to sputter and on a cold Thanksgiving night vs the Patriots, he entered Jets lore with the immortal play that will forever be known as...THE BUTTFUMBLE!

This whole fiasco culminated in the wonderful run of the estimable Geno Smith. In the 2013 draft, the Jets passed up on some talented players - Le'Veon Bell, Zach Ertz, Alec Ogletree - before zeroing in on Smith. Geno had a pretty good career at West Virginia, but because of rumors about his off-field antics, he fell to the 2nd round, still undrafted. The Jets would remedy that!

Jets fans had mixed emotions initially about this one, but eventually all solidly agreed that Geno was NOT the franchise savior. He went 13-16 in his career with Gang Green, was inconsistent with his play and had, um, dubious interactions with his teammates (a certain broken jaw...). This all led to a truncated Jets career, with the team releasing him after only three seasons.

Another year, another Jets draft mistake.

2

Gametime: Let the Pain Begin!

Drafts are just one area in which Jets fans can groan at all the mistakes and utter bone-headed moves made by their franchise. Unfortunately, that's just the tip of the iceberg. Once the draft is over, then it's time for the games to begin. One thing they can say with confidence: No other team has played anywhere near as many heartbreaking, frustrating, and unbelievably torturous games. The Jets lead the league...

It's Sunday, January 23rd 1983. We are at the Orange Bowl in Miami, Florida for the 1982 AFC Championship game. The Jets are in town taking on their hated rivals, the Miami Dolphins (By the way, this was BEFORE the Dan Marino disaster). The winner of this game will go on to face the Washington Redskins in Super Bowl XVII, being held in Pasadena, California. This game, however, is set for the unheard of start time of 1:00 p.m. (The practice had been for conference championship games to be held during "prime time", not in the early afternoon.)

This season has been somewhat interesting for both teams. Due to a player strike the season had been shortened to just 9 games. This gave every team, including the Jets, a better opportunity to make the playoffs and thus a run at that Super Bowl title. The Jets, led by Head Coach Walt Michaels, finished the strike-shortened year with a solid 6-3 record. They blew out the Cincinnati Bengals in the wild card game 44-17 and then eked out a 17-14 win vs. the (then) LA Raiders. So once again, Jets fans come into this game – the AFC Championship game – hopeful, maybe even a bit cocky, that despite all of the craziness, this season the Jets will FINALLY make it back to the Big One for the first time since the 1968 season.

The Dolphins, led by Hall of Fame coach Don Shula, come into this one with an impressive 7-2 record. They've had two convincing victories so far in the playoffs, a 28-13 win vs. the New England Patriots, and a 34-13 drubbing of the San Diego Chargers. It has been ten years since 1972, when the Dolphins went 17-0 becoming the only team in NFL history to go undefeated through the regular season and the playoffs. Clearly there is a lot riding on this one game for them as well!

Before the game even starts, there is a major controversy. There's a reason why this game is called, "The Mud Bowl"! During the week it had rained pretty hard in Miami. Putting the tarp down on the field, of course, would yield better playing conditions. But the night before, Don Shula decided to not have the field tarped! Thus when morning came, the field was incredibly muddy and wet. Jets coach Walt Michaels accuses Shula of purposely making the field muddy, an advantage for the Dolphins since they were a dominant running team and the Jets were a heavy passing team. Jets players, coaches, and fans feel that this game might not go their way.

They are pretty much right about that. The Jets gameplan is to use their dominant running attack, led by Freeman McNeil, to win them this game. The Dolphins are ready for that and are able to stuff the run all game long — aided, of course, by the muddy conditions. What happens next will make any Jets fan have another of the many strokes in their sporting life.

This whole game belongs to A.J. Duhe. Duhe is a linebacker for Miami who comes into this game with only 2 career interceptions. But in this one game alone, he proceeds to get not one, not two, but THREE interceptions, nearly single handedly punching the Dolphins ticket to the Super Bowl. He even scores one of the 2 touchdowns for Miami on a pick-six. A PICK-SIX!

A GUY WITH ONLY TWO CAREER INT'S HAS THREE IN THIS GAME ALONE, WITH ONE OF THEM BEING A PICK-SIX!?!? Alcohol consumption by Jets fans must have increased ten fold after this one...

Jets Quarterback Richard Todd has arguably the worst AFC Championship performance in NFL history. The Jets would go on and lose 14-0 and miss out on another golden opportunity for a chance at a Super Bowl.

Years pass, but the pain and agony remain the same for Jets fans. It's January 3rd, 1987. We are at Cleveland Municipal Stadium on a chilly afternoon in Cleveland, Ohio. It's the divisional round of the '87 playoffs between Our Heroes and the Cleveland Browns, two of the most snake-bitten franchises in NFL history.

The Jets, under head coach Joe Walton, come in with a 10-6 record in the regular season; however they had started 10-1 before going into one of their patented December swoons. The Browns led by Marty "Marty Ball" Schottenheimer come in as the favorites to go on to Super Bowl XXII, sporting an impressive 12-4 record. Both teams look to erase years of pain and misery by putting themselves just one win away from the Super Bowl.

The game would go on to become what is now referred

to, wistfully, as "The Marathon by the Lake". A four-hour grudge match that only the Jets could find a way to screw up.

The Jets are dominant throughout most of the game and it really looks like they will walk out of Cleveland with an easy victory and move on to the AFC Championship game. It seems even more likely this will happen after Freeman McNeil scores a TD that makes it 20-10 Jets with four minutes to go in the fourth quarter. But alas, as Jets fans have experienced far too many times, something goes amazingly wrong.

That something is Charley Steiner, the Jets radio play-by-play announcer. As Freeman goes in to score what should be the game winning touchdown, Steiner makes the now infamous call, "Touchdown! The Jets are gonna win this football game! The Jets are going to the AFC Championship"!

Well the Football Gods become very displeased with the Jets for Steiner's premature projection, and things begin to crumble. First, on the ensuing drive, Browns QB Bernie Kosar is hit late on a third down by Jets defensive end Mark Gastineau, keeping the drive alive. The Browns go down and score on a Kevin Mark rushing TD to make it 20-17 Jets with a little less than two minutes to go. Still

18

good , right Jets fans? That would be... no. After stopping the Jets on their next drive, the Browns get the ball back and with time expiring, Browns kicker Mark Moesley kicks a 22-yard field goal to send the game into overtime.

OVERTIME!!!

In a span of four minutes, the Jets have blown a two score lead and now have to go to OT. OK, OK, not to worry, we'll win it in overtime... At this point, every Jets fan is pretty much just waiting for the other shoe to drop. The Football Gods have decided to torture them by making them endure not one but two overtimes. OK, OK, not to worry, we'll win it in DOUBLE overtime...

But no. Remember, this is the Jets we're talking about...

Mark Moesley, who already has missed two field goal attempts in OT, trots onto the field to try a 27-yarder for the Browns and send THEM to the AFC Championship.

Moseley steps it off, and gets set, arms swinging by his side. The Browns O-line takes their stance. The snap... The kick is up...

Do I need to tell you what happened...?

So Jets fans, have you recovered from that one yet? I hope so, because we are far from over. Let's go eleven years later. It's September 6th, 1998. The Jets open their

season on the road in San Francisco against the 49ers.
The team and fans come in with high expectations in their
second season under former Super Bowl Champion head
coach Bill Parcells. Parcells had taken over the Jets in
1997 after they had finished with an embarrassing 1-15
record in '96. In '97, Parcels led the Jets to a 9-7 record
and just missed out on the playoffs on the last day of the
season, thanks to Barry Sanders of the Detroit Lions
breaking the 2000 yard rushing milestone against them in
the season finale, a 13-10 Lions victory. Regardless,
many Jets fans felt that the Jets were on the right flight
path and it was only going to get better from there.

This game goes back and forth with both teams getting
chances to pull away. With three seconds left in the
fourth quarter, Jets kicker John Hull kicks a game tying
field goal to mak

That's "most", but certainly not all! For one fan
already knows how this one will pe it 30 all forcing OT.
But despite the team's overtime travails, most Jets fans are
optimistic. lay out.

As the game goes into overtime, he calls a friend,
another long-suffering Jets fan. "After Hull made the
field goal, I called my neighbor - who wasn't home so I
left a message on his voicemail. I said, you watch, San

Francisco will get the ball inside the 5, but nonetheless will take it all the way down the field and score before the Jets even get a chance." Would that fan be a prophet. ?

Is the Pope a Patriots fan?

The 49ers get the ball to start overtime on their own 4 yard line. On the first play, the very first snap, 49ers halfback Garrison Hearst runs up the middle and scores on a 96-yard TD run to win the game for the Niners. Overtime over. Game over. Do the Jets win, though? Are you kidding?

As predicted, the Jets never even get a chance to touch the ball. The Jets at this point have become so predictable that their fans can see into the future on how they would lose games. Pessimism has morphed into clairvoyance...

Things only get more heart breaking later on the same season. The Jets shake off that frustrating loss at the beginning of the year and ride a tidal wave of emotion and success (and, oh by the way, excellent coaching) all the way to the AFC Championship game. Off they go to Denver to take on the defending Super Bowl champion Denver Broncos, who had defeated Brett Favre and his Green Bay Packers in a helicoptering way. This is the closest the Jets have gotten to the Super Bowl in awhile. This is also going to be Hall of Fame Broncos

Quarterback John Elway's last game at home in Denver. The Jets would love nothing more than to send Elway to retirement, blowing up his season a Mile High and moving on to the Super Bowl.

Throughout the first half, the game is a defensive struggle, with both teams going back and forth trying to get something, anything going offensively. At one point in the first half the Jets look like they are begging the Broncos to win this game, what with four fumbles and two interceptions thrown in, for "good" measure. Nonetheless, the
Jets are able to get the only score of the first half with a 32 yard field goal and lead the Broncos 3-0 at halftime. The Jets are sitting there, in the locker room, one half away from the Super Bowl...ONE HALF AWAY! WAIT – snap out of it, Jets fans! Something has to go wrong. And it does! Of course! You might be able to fool the wishful, but you can't fool Mother Nature!

In the second half, the wind gets stronger and stronger. And who does it really affect the most...?

The Jets start out the half strong, blocking a Broncos punt and recovering the ball at the Broncos' 1-yard line. On the very next play, Jets running back Curtis Martin runs it in for a Jets touchdown. Now the Jets lead 10-0,

22

and it's already into the 3rd quarter. Jets fans lick their chops and are starting to think of beautiful Miami, Florida (okay, well more beautiful than the LAST time...) where the 1999 Super Bowl would be held, an opportunity to bring that coveted Lombardi Trophy to New York! But not so fast, Jet fans! I think you know where this is headed...

On the ensuing drive, the Broncos finally get their offense going with a 47-yard catch by Ed McAffery. This in turn leads to Broncos fullback Howard Griffith scoring a touchdown and the Broncos getting back in the game, now only trailing 10-7. Not optimal, but still in the lead, Jets, right?

Then on the following kickoff, the wind catches the ball – not the Jets -and the Broncos recover deep in Jets territory.

The Jets hold, though, forcing Jason Elam to kick a field goal. In the span of about two minutes the Broncos have tied the game. Okay, okay, not great but not losing, either. Still a lot of time, right?RIGHT?

RIGHT!?

After the Jets go three-and-out (four, if you count a false start on first down), the Broncos get the ball back and kick another field goal to take their first lead at 13-10.

The Jets once again do nothing on offense, and the Broncos, in turn, once again score. This time it is a 31-yard touchdown to extend the Broncos lead to 20-10.

It's now late in the 3rd quarter. In a span of ten minutes, the Jets go from being UP by 10...TO BEING DOWN BY 10!!! The Jets continue to falter the rest of the game. The Broncos go on to win 23-10 and move on to the Super Bowl. For Jets fans, as the old saying goes, as noted above: You just can't fool Mother Nature!

For the next few years the Jets would go up and down in more ways than one. Parcells retires, Bill Belichick gets hired and leaves one day later. At least Al Groh has the courtesy of lasting a full season before bolting to his alma mater, the University of Virginia. A college team! The Jets struggle to find their next man in charge and then finally seem to get things together in 2004. For the next four years, under head coach Herm Edwards and the on-field leadership of quarterback Chad Pennington, the Jets have a very successful run, including one year, 2004, when they finish with a 10-6 record and reach the playoffs. The Jets beat the San Diego Chargers 20-17 on the road in the wild card game and earn the right to play Pittsburgh in the AFC Divisional Round game, in Steel City. The winner of this game will face the defending

Super Bowl Champ New England Patriots for the AFC title. ANOTHER opportunity for the Jets to put themselves in position to be one game away from the Super Bowl...

The game did not immediately go the Jets way. The Steelers jumped out to an early 10-0 and got those terrible towel fans into a frenzy. Then around the middle of the second quarter, after a Jets field goal, wide receiver Santana Moss returns a 75-yard punt for a crucial touchdown to tie the game at 10. The Jets were super pumped going into the locker room and they would take that momentum into the beginning of the third quarter. Jets cornerback Reggie Tongue picked off rookie QB Ben Roethlisberger for an 86 yard touchdown to give the Jets the lead!

Just like that, the Jets were once again on the verge of moving on in the postseason and putting themselves a heartbeat away from returning to the Super Bowl for the first time in nearly 40 years...

But this is the Jets, so things got interesting. At the beginning of the 4th quarter, the Steelers tied the game at 17 on a 4-yard shuffle pass to Hynes Ward. It's all good, though, because on the ensuing drive the Jets got down deep in Steelers territory, at the 28. They are within field goal range, There are two minutes left; make it and the Jets take the lead. All they would need is an almost certain Doug Brien go-ahead field goal...

NOPE! Brien misses a 47-yard field goal and the game remains tied! But that was to be expected, in all fairness. Fun fact – no opposition team had made a FG of more than 40 yards in the history of Heinz Field to that point.

Steelers fans are jubilant, thinking they have dodged the bullet. But no: Jets linebacker David Barrett picks off Big Ben on the very next play to set up the Jets drive at the Steelers 36 yard line.

In the next few plays, the Jets move the ball all the way down to the 23 yard line of the Steelers. Even if they were stopped right there, it would set up a 39 yarder for Brien.

Steeler's fans begin to stream out of the stadium. One Jets fan who was at the stadium was congratulated by them. "Wait!", the Jets fan said, "you obviously don't know the Jets!"

Herm Edwards had become famous for saying, "Hello? You play to win the game", but over the course of the next few plays, one could justifiably think well, he certainly isn't doing that here.! The Jets are stymied at the 23 yard line and so it looks like Brien will have that 39 yarder after all. But then, on third down, Mr. Play-to-Win-the-Game DECIDES TO GO CONSERVATIVE! He calls a KNEEL DOWN.

Now, Coach Edwards never seemed to get clock management right, but in this case, he also fails to grasp FIELD POSITION MANAGEMENT. See, whenever you take a kneel down you LOSE two YARDS.

So what's two yards among friends? Well, instead of attempting a 39 yarder, a kneel down would make it a 41 yarder. So what? Well, Herm, here's what (a little reminder that one would hope would be etched in the coach's brain): Again, NO OPPOSING TEAM HAD EVER MADE A FIELD GOAL IN HEINZ FIELD LONGER THAN 40 YARDS.

Of course, there is nothing written that says somebody, some day won't break that barrier. But why your team, Herm? And why now? Why not save the honor for, say, an early regular season contest? Why roll the dice in the playoffs?

And, um, with the Jets? The JETS, Herm – THE JETS.

Wide left. JUUUUST wide left. In fact, a couple of yards closer in and it probably would have sneaked through the uprights. Two yards, Herm...

Wide left.

Somehow, yet again, the Jets had blown their golden opportunity. They had had not one, but TWO chances to win the game ("you play to win the game", remember, Herm?) in regulation, but blew them both. Now the game has to go into overtime.

The Steelers win the coin toss in OT and proceed to go on a 13-play 72 yard drive to set up what looks to be a surefire 33-yard field goal by Steelers kicker Jeff Reid. GUESS WHAT? YOU READY!?!? He knocks it through and the Steelers win 20-17 and move on to the AFC Championship. Had you played to win the game, Herm? No! You just played to LOSE the game.

"Only" seven years later ("only" is a looonnnggg time for a fan, especially a Jets fan), on January 23rd, 2011, the Jets found themselves back in the spotlight. After their remarkable run to the AFC Championship the year prior (ended by Payton Manning - no shame there), the Men in Green fought their way back to the championship game for a second straight year. This time, they head to that familiar place, Heinz Field in Pittsburgh. Jets Head Coach Rex Ryan was clearly making his mark in Jets lore with two consecutive trips to the AFC title game in his first two seasons as an NFL Head Coach. He brought energy, grit, a lot of interesting storylines – and a commitment to, and emphasis on, defense.

The Jets come in with two big wins already in the playoffs against two bona fide Hall of Fame quarterbacks. They got their revenge from last years' AFC title game against Peyton Manning and the Colts, then went to Foxboro and beat Tom Brady, Bill Belichick and the Patriots. Now they are one win away – yet again - from the Super Bowl! Sound familiar Jet fans?

The Jets had loaded up for this season by adding Ladainian Tomlinson at running back and Super Bowl 43 MVP and former Steeler Santonio Holmes. Most importantly, though, they also upgraded their defense, including adding future Hall of Famer Jason Taylor, linebacker from the hated Dolphins.

The Steelers come into the game as one of the hottest teams in football. They had ground out a 31-24 win vs. the Ravens in the Divisional Round to get to this point. Now they are looking to once again play spoilers to the Jets run at getting back to the Superbowl for the first time since '68. Steelers Head Coach Mike Tomlin is looking to make a run of his own – a second Super Bowl title in four years. Something's gotta give...

The Steelers come out like a house on fire and

dominate right from the get-go. The offense clicks immediately and they lead 24-3 at the half. As for the Jets, where is that vaunted defense? Where is the "ground and pound" that Rex brags so much about? They just couldn't seem to get anything going and looked worse than they had looked all year long. The half climaxed with a fumble by Jets QB Mark Sanchez which was returned for a Pittsburgh touchdown giving them the aforementioned 24-3 lead.

It is showing all the signs of a very disappointing finish to another heartbreaking season of Jets football. Then, the tide shifted. Whether it was the feeling from last year motivating the team or Rex Ryan losing ten pounds from his halftime speech to his players, the bottom line was that the Jets wake up in the second half.

On the opening drive, Sanchez finds, of all people, Santonio Holmes for a touchdown that makes it 24-10 just 3 minutes into the 3rd quarter. Just like that, there is life in Gang Green. Now the defense – the pride of the team and the coach – finally shows up. The Jets force an interception on the Steelers next drive and get the ball back with 7:42 left in the third and still only down by 14.

But then the Jets proceed to go on an 8 minute drive to start the fourth quarter which is a huge cause for concern considering you need two scores just to tie the game. Still, they move the ball all the way down to the 1-yard line and have not one, not two, not even three, BUT FOUR CHANCES TO SCORE...NO DICE!. So with just a little over seven minutes left, the Steelers regain the ball on their own 1 yard line and still up by 14.

It's over right?

Well not necessarily. On the very next play, the Jets force a safety (DE-FENSE! DE-FENSE!) and get the ball back again, this time trailing by 12. The Jets chew up much less clock on this drive AND they score! Sanchez finds Jerricho Cotchery for the TD and all of the sudden, they are only down 24-19 with 3:06 left in the game. All they need is one more stop on defense and a touchdown on offense and they are in the SuperBowl! THE SUPERBOWL!

Alas, Jets fans, you know how this one pans out. 3rd and 6 for the Steelers at the Jet 40-yard line with 1:57 left in the game. Jets have 0 timeouts but still have a chance to get the stop. Big Ben scrambles to his right, hesitates, and then...finds Antonio Brown for a first down. Rex Ryan throws his headset in disgust as the Jets fall 24-19 and miss out once again, one win away from the Super Bowl. Agony, thy name is Sexy Rexy.

You still with me Jets fans? Good, because I have one more game to talk about. January 3rd, 2016, in the cold, snowy Ralph Wilson Stadium in Buffalo, New York. The Jets come in with a 10-5 record needing just "one more win" (Where have we heard THAT before...?) to make the playoffs. Head Coach Todd Bowles, in his first year with the Jets, has guided an electrifying offense led by Ryan "Fitzmagic" Fitzpatrick and his 29 touchdown passes and wide receiver Brandon Marshall, to a ten win season and possible playoff berth.

The Buffalo Bills come in at 7-8, well out of the playoffs. The one advantage that the Bills have going into this game is their new head coach...Rex Ryan. Yes! Sexy Rexy! A year after he was fired by these same Jets, he became the Bills top guy He would love nothing more than to ruin his former team's chances at making the playoffs.

Thus it would be easy to understand that Rex Ryan had all the emotion and got the Bills up for this game!

Todd Bowles is the complete opposite. He has no emotion on the sideline, treating this game like any other regular season matchup. Right there is where everything starts to fall apart.

The Jets go down by 13, early in the second quarter,

and already look defeated. But then they respond quickly. Fitzpatrick finds Brandon Marshall for his 30th TD pass of the season and cuts the Bills lead to 13-7 with 9:39 to go in the first half. Anyone's game!

The teams trade scores but the Jets miss opportunities to narrow the gap by missing a tough 40 yard field goal. Then things get really heated.

With the Jets trailing 19-10 after both teams trade field goals, Fitzpatrick finds Eric Decker for a touchdown to cut the deficit to two, 19-17 Bills with a little over one minute left in the third quarter. After they force a punt, the Jets drive down deep in Bills territory, at which point the legend of "Fitzception" is born. Fitzpatrick throws a huge interception in the Bills endzone and the Bills take over still up by 2 with 10:43 left in the game. The Bills are then able to chew up clock and kick a field goal. 22-17, Bills, with 6:54 to play.

The Jets get the ball back needing a touchdown to win the game and make the playoffs. THE PLAYOFFS!

But - "Fitzception" strikes again!

Fitzpatrick throws another interception and the Bills once again get the ball back, looking to ice the game. Yet somehow, the Jets find themselves with a THIRD chance to win, with 30 seconds left But "Fitzception" puts the final nail in the coffin, throwing a THIRD interception to end the game. The Jets lose 22-17 and miss out on the playoffs. Had Todd Bowles gotten his team emotionally ready for this game, maybe the Jets win and make the playoffs. Emotion is everything.

But right now, the only emotion is the empty feeling of loss. Of missing out on a big opportunity.

Yet again.

3

Killer Plays

Jets fans, regrettably, will always remember those heart-breaking losses that ruined the Jets many chances to win another Super Bowl over the years - or even participate in one. However, sometimes it's not the entire game that ends it for them. Sometimes it's just one single - and singular - play that changes, not just the trajectory of a game, and not just a season, but the future of the entire franchise - forever.

December 24th, 2011. It's Christmas Eve at Metlife Stadium. The Jets, sitting at 8-6, are hoping to not find any coal in their stocking the next morning and make the playoffs for a third straight year, getting back to the AFC Championship once again as they had done the previous two years - but this time reaching that elusive Super Bowl.

Their opponent on this day is their crosstown rivals - some would say big brothers - The New York Giants. The Giants come in needing to win their final two games to make the playoffs. The only way they can do that is to win the division outright; no wild card can come out of it. As for the Jets? They need to win both of their last two games just to get into postseason. This one is certainly an early Christmas present for football fans!

The Jets get off to a good start on their first drive of the game as Mark Sanchez finds fullback Josh Baker for a 6-yard touchdown to put the Jets in front 7-0 halfway through the first quarter. The Jets throw the ball quite a lot in this game. Offensive coordinator Brian Schottenheimer wants to hurt the Giants defense with the passing game. The Jets defense dominates the Giants in the majority of the first half and all the Giants could do is muster a field goal to cut the deficit to 7-3. It seems to be looking good for the Jets to get some huge Big Apple bragging rights - oh, and keep their playoff hopes alive. Then, as it always pretty much seems to go, things begin to fall apart...

The Giants, on 3rd and 10 from their own 1 yard with 2:27 left in the 1st half, throw the ball! Eli Manning finds Victor Cruz who jukes two defenders and breaks a 99-yard touchdown to give the Giants the lead at 10-7. Jets fans are stunned and groan, knowing all too well what will happen next.

After the Jets get the ball and drive down into field goal range, Nick Folk proceeds to miss the field goal attempt just as the clock expires to conclude the first half.

The Jets go into the locker room down 3 and looking dejected. Most other teams will bounce back and come out confident in the 2nd half. However, St. Nicholas has other plans for Gang Green.

Late in the 3rd quarter, the Giants, deep in Jets territory score again on an Ahmad Bradshaw touchdown run. He also lowers the shoulder on Jets safety Rodney Poole, knocking him out of the game. That hit pretty much symbolizes how Jets fans are feeling. They are getting beaten up and knocked out by their big brother.

Later on, with 9 minutes remaining in the contest, Mark Sanchez, at the Giants 2-yard line, fumbles the ball and the Giants recover in the endzone for a touchback The Jets lose any momentum they had. (This is pre-buttfumble, understand...) The Jets keep throwing the ball and they would go on to score on a Mark Sanchez touchdown run to cut the deficit to just 6 with 7:24 remaining. Then, with about 6 minutes left in the game and the Jets still only down 20-14, Sanchez throws an interception to seal the game for Big Blue. Giants go on and score 9 more points and take the battle of New York 29-14. The Jets passed 59 times in the game! 59 TIMES! None were more...THAN 16 YARDS!

The real story, some say, behind the excessive amount

of pass attempts was that Rex was so obsessed with "ground and pound" that it made Schottenheimer disgruntled. Brian knew that Sanchez was a long passer and the Jets O should have integrated more of that into their offense. Rex, though, was insistent in keeping Sanchez pegged to short dump offs. So Schottenheimer - in his second to last game as Jets OC, the theory goes - did this as a conscious parting shot at Rex - shoving dump offs down Rex's throat. Sanchez was always out-of-character in Rex's version of the Jets O. That part is the real story - It's not that the Jets got away from what they had done. It's that Schottenheimer believed the Jets had become too one-dimensional and were squandering Sanchez's real talent.

So much for dime-store psychological analysis. The facts, though, were these: This game would propel the Giants all the way to the Super Bowl, even winning it against the favored Patriots. As for the Jets, they finish the year at 8-8 and miss out on the playoffs YET AGAIN, on the final day of the season.

Unfortunately for Jets fans, things get a whole lot worse just 10 months later...

November 22, 2012. Thanksgiving night and week 12 of the 2012-13 NFL season. While many people and their families are recovering from getting stuffed with turkey, gravy, and cranberry sauce, Jets fans file into Metlife Stadium to see the 4-6 Jets take on their hated rivals and division leading 7-3 New England Patriots. It certainly had been a difficult year for the Jets and their fans. They were coming off failing to make the playoffs the year before after back-to-back AFC Championship appearances. Going into this game tonight, there they sat with a sub .500 record: Jets fans are not pleased.

So not pleased that they begin to call for quarterback Mark Sanchez to be benched and replaced with first-year Jet Tim Tebow! TIM TEBOW!?!? "Tebowtime", had come to the Big Apple in the offseason. Many Jets fans suspected Jets owner Woody Johnson had signed Tebow as a publicity stunt. Be that as it may, fans now wanted to see that Tebow magic come to life before the season was completely lost. But despite the fans' impatience, Rex Ryan opted to stay with Sanchez and the game began.

The game started off with a bang. If you think that means "in a good way for Jets fans" then this book isn't for you. Sanchez throws a pass deep in Patriots territory on their second drive of the game. The pass is picked off by Patriots Defensive Back Steve Gregory. The Pats go down the field and score on a Tom Brady touchdown pass to give New England the early 7-0 lead. From there, the teams lock into a defensive struggle until 5 minutes into the 2nd quarter.

The Jets have the ball once again in field goal range and run the ball with Running Back Bilal Powell on 3rd and short. They don't get it. You would think the Jets would just kick the field goal and get on the board, right?

Well, that doesn't happen. The Jets go for it on 4th down and run THE EXACT SAME PLAY! This time with Running Back Shonn Greene. He gets hit by Patriots linebacker Brandon Spikes and fumbles the ball! Steve Gregory, (the same guy who intercepted Sanchez earlier) picks up the ball and returns it deep into Jets territory. The Pats score again and now it's 14-0 Patriots with 9:45 left in the 1st half.

Jets fans, please stop reading right here if you know what happens next. On 1st and 10 from their own 31-yard line, they run a misdirection play. However, Sanchez turns around the wrong way and realizes he is alone with the ball. He then proceeds to run straight into Jets offensive lineman Brandon Moore's, um, posterior (unfortunately, Moore was not equipped with optional back-up sound) and fumbles the ball. Steve Gregory, (AGAIN), picks up the ball and runs it in for a touchdown

41

to make it 21-0 Patriots.

Thus the infamous "ButtFumble" is born...

The Jets would go on to lose that game 49-19 and finish the year 6-10. Mark Sanchez may have achieved great accomplishments early in his Jet career, but he will always be remembered by Jets fans as Mr. ButtFumble. One play changed the course of one man's career and destroyed the hope that the Jets had in the future with "The Sanchize".

When you hear the name Paul Hackett, you don't really think too much of it right? Most people wouldn't even know who he was. However, for Jets fans, when they hear that name, instead of ground and pound all they can do is moan and groan.

Paul Hackett was the Jets offensive coordinator between 2001-2004. He was known for being a conservative coach and boy did he live up to expectations, especially in the last two years of that period.

This man was even given a 2nd chance with the Jets in 2003 after Herm Edwards had fired his defensive coordinator Ted Cotrell and was considering firing Hackett as well. He stayed on only if he promised to be more creative. Whelp, nothing happened and even before Edwards could fire him, Hackett resigned and left the Jets after that 2004 debacle.

What "debacle", you might ask? All you have to do is refer to earlier in this chapter - the 2004 divisional round game vs the Steelers. He was the guy who ran the ball 3 times up the middle to set up a long 40 plus yard field goal attempt to try and win the game for the Jets, despite the fact that up to that point no opposing team had ever kicked a 40+ yard FG in that stadium. They of course missed the kick and the Jets went on to lose the game.

It is safe to say that Hackett will go down as one of the worst and most incompetent coaches the Jets had, ever.

But the question remains - why WAS Hackett on the hot seat to begin with? To find the answer to that question, we have to delve into the matter of...

4

Killer Fans

When we think of sports, we think of not just the players and teams that are involved, but the fans that support the teams. There are passionate, loyal, and super supportive fans who always remain positive and stick by their team no matter what.

And then there are Jets fans...

Can there be a more pessimistic and snake bitten group of fans for a team than the Jets? With a fan base comes iconic fans with names and incidences that stand out in sports fan history.

When you hear the name Edwin M. Anzalone, you may or may not know off the top of your head who that person is. To most, he sounds just like a regular person like you and me. However, to many Jets fans, he is the most iconic fan in Jets history. He goes by the nickname - a term of reverence, really - "Fireman Ed". He would go to every Jets home game and begin with the famous, "J-E-T-S, JETS, JETS, JETS", chant. Everyone has heard, in one way or another, this chant and seen Fireman Ed do his thing, He would wear a fireman helmet, resplendent in

44

Jets colors and appointed with Jets regalia, standing among the crowd of Jets fans, game in, game out.

Unfortunately, after years and years of inciting support for the team, this Jets icon was suddenly absent from Jets games. Was his absence due to health reasons or his duties as a firefighter? As with everything that involves the Jets, the reason is not so understandable.

We have to go back to Thanksgiving evening, November 22, 2012. That date may not ring a bell, but it will ever rankle in the mind of Jets fans as "The Butt Fumble Game"...

Immediately after that play, Anzalone actually got up from his seat and proceeded to walk right out of Metlife Stadium. As he was leaving the game, he stated to the crowd of Jets fans around him that he would never again do those chants at Jets games. He had given up on the team.

This broke the hearts of many a diehard Jets fan who, over time, had built a relationship with this man, if only from afar. Many people worried and wondered if they would ever see or hear from Fireman Ed ever again...

Then, in Week 2 of the 2018 season, Fireman Ed made his return to Metlife Stadium to do the Jets chant, since the team was showing a lot of promise under the leadership of rookie quarterback Sam Darnold.

This is the type of loyal, dedicated and hopeful fan that this team has engendered over the years.

Of course, this is also the team that can drive even the most loyal, dedicated and hopeful fan to the breaking point...Go back to the 1995 NFL Draft. Many Jets fans flocked to Radio City Music Hall, certain of watching the Jets make the best draft decision in their team's recent history. Warren Sapp, the standout defensive end, and future Hall of Famer from the University of Miami, was the big prize. Sapp had been dealing with false rumors about drug use, which resulted in him falling more and more in the draft. Jets fans got more and more excited with each pick that went by. They were realizing that the best player in the draft was falling all right - right into the hands of the Jets.

Then came the #9 overall pick...The Jets. Jets fans chant, "We want Sapp! We want Sapp"! NFL Commissioner Paul Tagliabue walks up to the podium and intones:, "With the 9th pick in the first round, The New York Jets select..." Jets fans nearly squeal in excited anticipation – Warren Sapp, Warren Sapp!

"Tight End from Penn State, Kyle Brady."

A shock wave flows through the crowd. Jets fans are

in shock, ESPN is in shock, EVEN KYLE BRADY IS IN SHOCK! How could the Jets have taken a tight end?? NFL Analyst Joe Theismann, himself in shock, says that this pick made no sense and wonders aloud if the Jets were going to a 2 TE system.

Poor Kyle Brady! He goes up to the podium to a chorus of boos. One Jets fan recalled saying at the draft, "This is a bad dream. Thirty years of lousy picks and lousy football". Kyle Brady would go on to become a solid tight end, but not a Hall of Famer. Not a Warren Sapp! Jets fans still to this day can never forget this draft, what might have been... how they could've had a Hall of Fame player over a tight end...

The 2013 NFL Draft was another "interesting" time for Jets fans. They were hoping that the team would look for yet another big name defensive player that could help reshape the defense to recapture past glory. Fans traveled to Metlife Stadium for the Jets draft party. Everyone was having a great time, until the #13th overall pick...The Jets had already taken Dee Milliner with the #9th selection and now the hope was that they would add another big name, one Kyle Long. Commissioner Roger Goodell again walked to the podium:, "With the 13th selection in the 2013 NFL Draft, The New York Jets select...Sheldon

Richardson, Defensive End, Missouri."

Now, Sheldon Richardson turned out to be a solid player. But that day, in the eyes of many Jets fans, it was yet another shocking and unnecessary pick by the Jets. One Jets fan was so outraged that he led a chant at the draft party, "I swear to God we suck! WE SUCK! WE SUCK! WE SUCK! WE SUCK! WE SUCK!"

See, Jets fans are so shell shocked by terrible draft picks, that they cannot easily recognize a good one when it happens.

The Jets have one of the most iconic uniforms in NFL history. They had worn the same uniforms when they won Super Bowl III. They went to three AFC Championship Games in those uniforms. Jets fans will always love and appreciate them. Unfortunately, nothing good ever lasts in Jets land. The Jets changed their uniform in 1978 to a dark green helmet that just reads Jets. There are fans who loved them, but they did little to help with the success of the Jets. Then they changed them back to the original kelly green in 1990.

Then it's April 5th, 2019. It seems that April Fools Day has lasted a few days longer for Jets fans. Let's take a step back: The team announced the year prior that they would be changing their uniforms and starting, "A new

ERA of Jets Football" (How many times have you heard THAT one, Jets fans?) The team decided to reveal them at the Gotham Theater in New York City.

Thus the many Jets fans who are gathered there are anxious and excited to see what they look like. After a lot of hoopla, it's finally time to unveil them. Sam Darnold, Quarterback for the Jets, walks out in the new duds and is greeted with only a half cheering crowd. Some fans can't believe it. The team had gone back to kelly green all right...But with a combination of green jerseys and white pants and a kelly green helmet. They also included all white uniforms and an all black, "Gotham", uniform.

Truly, some Jet fans were shocked, disappointed, embarrassed, and angry. In reaction, many Jets fans went to social media to express their opinions. One stated, "They've played like a high school team long enough. Might as well dress like one". Another via Twitter said, "They look like jerseys for an arena league team". One fan couldn't help roasting a different league in the process: "I thought the AAF (Alliance of American Football) was dead". Only the Jets could do this to their own fan base. No luck of the Irish for Jets fans.

But at least one thing Jets fans can say that they have never done is initiate a massive snowball barrage, FROM

THE STANDS AGAINST YOUR OWN TEAM, like fans of that other New York Football team that we know. As bad as Jets fandom got, Jets fans didn't fly a banner over the stadium showing their discontent... Altho maybe it's just because they didn't have the money to hire one.
But snowballs??

What's a snowball? We've all made the flimsy things of the fluffy stuff and thrown them at our girlfriends or boyfriends. Maybe, maybe, you packed one really, really hard with ice to throw at your kid brother - maybe he cries - Don't you dare tell Mom! You warn...
I mean, after all, it's a snowball! A SNOW-BALL!
Fans can be forgiven for not being the sharpest physics students, understood. This is FOOTBALL, after all, not Bronx Science.

But there's this thing called gravity. And gravity means acceleration. And acceleration means force - which, from the upper deck means a snowball thrown from up there is gonna hit someone at field level with a LOT of force. Potentially DEADLY force.

Which is a big deal when you're on field level, on the receiving end. And, given the injuries that can result (and 15 injuries resulted, along with 14 arrests and 175 ejections) - and their seriousness - it's gonna be something that will be a big deal to the cops as well…

Now, your team is playing poorly, has all season. The frustration is understandable. But at least have the good sense to not help the cops find you. At least have the good sense to STAY OFF THE BACK PAGE OF THE TABLOIDS!

But no - So WHAT if I'm on the back page? So easy to identify me? So what?

Well, how about an arrest for assault with a deadly weapon??

Jets fans may be disgruntled but... Giants fans GOT ARRESTED.

(To be fair, the next day was a Jets game, and no alcohol was sold or permitted in the Stadium... That's GIANTS Stadium, as the Jets did not even have their own stadium...)

All that being said, Jets fans always find a way to stand out in any NFL fan crowd. Snowballs notwithstanding, there aren't many teams even close to being similar to Jets fans. Suffering, thy name is "Jets fan".

5

Gang Green for Real

In any sport, no matter what it is, there will be injuries. Sometimes they are not too serious, and other times they can be season- or even career-ending. There are all sorts of injuries that have different effects on players, teams, and fans. But when it comes to injuries, the Jets have suffered some of the most ironic and agonizing injuries, not just their own team, but to other teams. And in doing so, they have created a legend with decades of futility.

We start with, "Broadway" Joe Namath. The man who, as we all know, is responsible for guaranteeing the Jets a win in Super Bowl III and fulfilling that guarantee by knocking off the heavily favored Baltimore Colts. Things really looked like they were on the upswing after that for Namath and the Jets. Then, like Joe Namath's knees, it all fell apart.

To be fair, when Namath came into the American Football League in 1965, he already had bad knees from his time at Alabama. When, after the Jets drafted him with by far the largest offer in pro football history to that point, he had surgery on his knees in New York, the doctors told him he could only play 4 years. Well, Namath defied the odds and ended up playing 13 years. However, it came with a heavy price. Altho knee injuries kept him hobbled for much of his first two seasons, his knees really began to fail him in 1971 - and kept getting worse and worse. It got so bad that he was eventually released by the Jets in 1976 and finished his career with the Los Angeles Rams. Were these injuries a punishment to Namath for winning the Super Bowl? The price he had to pay for a "deal with the devil"? Jets fans still wonder...

Things only got worse for injured Jets Quarterbacks. The transition from Namath was made easier when the team drafted QB Richard Todd in the first round of the 1976 NFL Draft. Many Jets fans had high hopes for another big time Alabama quarterback. He got the chance to start right away at the age of 23 and many people were excited.

Unfortunately, things never met such high expectations. Todd suffered several knee injuries in his time in New York and the team never seem to get things going under him. Every time he got healthy, it seemed like the next game he would go down again. This led to a period of mediocrity for the Jets and the team suffered mightily from it. Todd finished his career with the New Orleans

Saints as the Jets once again had to go and find their franchise QB.

Vinny Testaverde had one of the most classic misfortunes in team history. It was a beautiful day at Giants Stadium as the Jets faced off against the rival New England Patriots in week 1 of the 1999 season. The Jets, who were coached by Bill Parcells and Defensive Coordinator Bill Belichick (wherever have we heard that name...?) had come off losing in the AFC Championship game the previous year. The team had high expectations going into 99 and Vinny Testaverde was the leading man of a balanced offensive attack with Curtis Martin at halfback. It seemed all set up for J-E-T-S success!

On the very first drive of the contest, Testaverde found Reggie Anderson for a touchdown and the emotions and excitement were at an all time high! 1999 would be the year of the Jets! Then it all fell apart, literally.

With a little over 7 minutes left in the 1st half and the Jets down 10-7, Testaverde handed the ball off to Curtis Martin who fumbled the ball and then recovered it for a loss. Just like that, the cameras shifted to Testaverde rolling around on the turf, holding his left leg. Nobody knew how, but the Gang Green turf had gotten Testaverde's leg, injuring him severely.

Testaverde had been an iron man - he was never bothered by injuries, nor had he lost any significant time to them. But then, on a play that didn't even involve him, he went down, and wouldn't get up for the rest of the season.

It was later reported that Testaverde had ruptured his achilles and was done for the season. Parcells then proceeded to start Rick Mirer at QB. The same QB who was a former #2 overall pick by Seattle and became a journeyman quarterback who had already proven that he couldn't be the guy. Then, after seven weeks of futility, Parcells put in undrafted quarterback out of Rutgers (and now Jets analyst), Ray Lucas. He took over in week 8 and propelled the Jets to a 6-3 record in his time. However, the Jets never recovered from the poor start from Mirer and stumbled to an 8-8 record and just out of the playoffs.

Testaverde never was the same QB, Parcells retired, and Belichick? Well, you know THAT story. What could have happened had Vinny been healthy? Could the Jets have won a Super Bowl? Would Parcells have stayed? Would Belichick have never gone to the Patriots? We will never know and Jets fans are left to wonder forever.

Then we have Chad Pennington. The Jets had taken him with the #18th overall selection in the 2000 NFL

Draft. He was picked ahead of a skinny kid out of Michigan who was taken with the #199th pick by the Patriots, some kid by the name of Tom Brady. Pennington got off to a very good start in his career. In 2002 he replaced Vinny Testaverde and led the 1-4 Jets to a 9-7 record and an AFC East title. He even defeated Peyton Manning in a playoff game 41-0. The Jets looked as if they had found their man who would lead them back to the Super Bowl. Alas, it was soon all torn away...

Pennington suffered his first major injury in the 4th preseason game of the 2003 season vs the Giants. Linebacker Brandon Short hit Pennington's throwing hand, causing him to lose balance and fall to the turf in an awkward way. Pennington ended up enduring a fracture-dislocation and missed the first 5 games of the year. Despite returning, Pennington never was the same and the team finished 6-10. Pennington's injuries then began to pile up.

The very next year in 2004, he injured his right rotator cuff in Week 6 vs the Buffalo Bills after a 5-0 start. He would return 4 weeks later to guide the Jets to the divisional round of the playoffs. But after the season, Pennington would go through the first of two major rotator cuff surgeries in the span of six months. He then lost the zip on the ball when he threw it and the Jets began to lose patience. After 3 mediocre seasons, the Jets released Pennington, having fallen in love with and proposed marriage to former Packers quarterback Brett Favre. This where things really get hot and heavy.

The "Gunslinger of all gunslingers" led the Jets to an 8-3 record. By Thanksgiving the experts were proclaiming the Jets as the best team in the NFL.

Then HE got injured...

The Jets rival, the Miami Dolphins, signed Pennington the very next day after his release. Both teams met up in week 17 of the 2008 season at Giants Stadium with not only the division on the line, but the last playoff spot. Pennington thrived against his former team, while the Jets and hobbled Favre stumbled. Pennington threw for 200 yards and 2 touchdowns to lead the Dolphins to a 24-17 victory , winning the division and making the postseason. Pennington won his 2nd Comeback Player of the Year award. Brett Favre retired - and then UN-retired! - a few months later and the Jets were left without any QB at all. Talk about being left at the altar.

There is one injury however, that stands above all the others. This one is so bad it not only doesn't even involve someone on the Jets, but it changed the course of one franchise and the birth of an NFL dynasty. It came in week 2 of the 2001 season. The Jets traveled to Foxborough, Massachusetts to face their rivals, the New England Patriots and their franchise quarterback, Drew Bledsoe. The teams got into a defensive struggle with the Jets clinging on to a 10-3 lead late in the fourth. It was looking like a well earned Jets defensive victory against a defensive guru, right? One who also had left the Jets at the altar, not unlike Favre would do a few years later...

Well, let's just say that whenever Mo Lewis' name comes up, Jets fans practically keel over and die!

On a 3rd and 10 for the Patriots from their own 18 yard line, Drew Bledsoe ran to his right, out of the pocket and was going towards the first down marker. As he proceeded to run out of bounds just short of the 1st, Jets linebacker Mo Lewis hit Bledsoe above his waist and knocked him out of the game. Bledsoe was done for the game. Who replaced him you might ask? Oh, just some 6th round quarterback from Michigan. I think his name was...Tom Brady. The Jets would go on to win that game, but the damage had been done.

Bledsoe suffered a sheared blood vessel in his chest as a result of Lewis' hit and nearly died. Thankfully he survived and played several more seasons in the NFL -

just not with the Patriots. You see, turns out Tom Brady could actually play. YES! THIS SKINNY, STRING BEAN OF A KID ACTUALLY WAS KICKING MOFOBO ALL OVER THE FIELD!!! Brady would take Bledsoe's starting job and never look back. He would go on to win (as of the time of this writing) SIX Super Bowl titles and create one of the greatest dynasties in sports history!

As for the Jets? Well, they are still paying for Mo Lewis' big hit. To this day, the Jets will never forget September 23rd, 2001. A day that will live in infamy in Jets history. Brady becomes the best, the Jets become grotesque.

6

This Is Not a Carousel That You'd Want to Ride

When it comes to coaching, no one understands that better than the Jets. A team that has had one of the more dizzying coaching carousels in NFL history. Each coach has a personality, a shtick, an idea of what they are doing. When it comes to Jets coaches, not only have they been failures (only two coaches have had winning records with the team, Parcells and Groh, but together they coached the team for a total of 3 seasons), but they have been at the helm of some of the most inconsistent coaching performances that have ever been witnessed in football. This is certainly a merry-go-round that you wouldn't want to get on any time soon.

It seemed that after Super Bowl III, the Jets really struggled to find a replacement for Weeb Ewbank, who understood what it took to succeed and put his team in the best position to win. So it made sense when they hired the man who was in charge of the defense in '68, Walt Michaels. Many Jets fans thought that he would be the man to guide the Jets to more glory. At first, he brought positivity and hope, guiding the Jets to the playoffs in 1981, the first time since 68. The year after that, he took the team to the AFC Championship game!

Everything was looking great, and then it ended. Right after that season, Michaels abruptly retired saying that he needed time away from football. The emotional strain was too much for him and he also wanted to spend more time with his ill mother. Michaels would never return to coach the Jets again. It was certainly sickening for Jets fans to see such promise leave.

The man to replace him was Joe Walton, the offensive coordinator for the Jets what was then the past two seasons. Walton was also another Beaver Falls product, just like Joe Namath, so many thought that some old Monongahela magic would come back and help the Jets. Instead, what the fans got was so-so. Walton guided the Jets to the playoffs only twice between 1983 and 1989. He posted a 53-57-1 record in his time. Jets fans were glad to see him go when he left the Jets to become offensive coordinator of the Pittsburgh Steelers in 1990. Mediocrity, thy name is Walton.

The Jets would then hire a relatively unknown man in Bruce Coslet in 1990. Coslet really had no chance right off the bat to get the Jets to the next level. He took over a

4-12 team and only got a little bit better. The Jets went 6-10 his first year. The next year in 1991, the Jets scratched and clawed their way into the wild card game vs the Houston Oilers in which they would go on to lose. It would turn out to be the only playoff appearances Coslet would get in his time in New York. The Jets would have two more mediocre seasons in 92 and 93. The Jets record was 12-20 in Coslet's last year. The team never got going. They were so desperate that they traded for Coslet's former QB and Bengal trailblazer Boomer Esiason. I guess the Jets really wanted Coslet to succeed. However, success didn't follow Coslet or the Jets and the team fired him after the 1993 season.

The next hire maybe one of the worst hires not just in Jets history, but possibly in NFL history. Who might you ask? Well it's none other than the legendary man himself...Rich Kotite. Yes! Rich Kotite was hired in 1995 after the Jets fired future USC great Pete Carroll, who was fired after just one albeit mediocre season. JUST ONE SEASON!

Anyway, Kotite was hired the next year and came to the Jets with a pretty average record of 36-28 in his time as the head coach in Philadelphia. The book on him from Philly fans and players was not very good. But did that stop the Jets from taking him?

In Philly he struggled to get the best out of his superstar quarterback, Randall Cunningham. He lasted several bad seasons with only one playoff spot before he was let go. Jets fans to this day scratch their heads and wonder just what the Jets were thinking when they made this hire. Some hoped that maybe playing for his hometown team would spark new life in him and the Jets...sadly, that turned out not to be the case at all. The Jets, to put it bluntly, had two of the worse seasons in both franchise and NFL history. When I say they were bad, that doesn't do it justice. THEY WERE PURE AND UTTER HOT GARBAGE!

The team would go on to have records of 3-13 in 1995 and, not to be outdone by that debacle, 1-15 in 1996. Can you believe that!?!? A guy who was pretty bad somehow got worse with a completely different team! Well, believe it folks, it really happened. Any Jets fan can tell you – oh baby, it really happened! It got so bad that the Jets didn't even fire Kotite and he ended up retiring just before the last game of the 96 season. He will also be remembered for drafting Tight End Kyle Brady over Future Hall of Famer Warren Sapp. Hall. Of. FAMER!

Things seemed to be at an all time low for the Jets and

their fans. Then, all of the sudden everything changed – and for the better!. Bill Parcells, the man who won 2 Super Bowls with the Giants and New England was brought in in 1997 to take over the Jets. Parcells also brought in the man behind the great Giants defense of those Superbowl championship teams, Bill Belichick, to be Defensive Coordinator. This immediately brought new enthusiasm and excitement, and it showed on the field.

The Jets would finish with a 9-7 record in Parcells first year. Not enough for the postseason maybe, but WAY better than 1-15! This was one of the single greatest team turnarounds in NFL history. The team would take a bigger step forward in 1998. They would finish with a record of 12-4 for the 2nd best record in the AFC. They would beat the Patriots at home in the Divisional Round and put themselves one win away from the Super Bowl!

However, the team would lose in heartbreaking and disappointing fashion against the defending Super Bowl Champion Denver Broncos. It ended a great year that only increased the expectations going into the 1999 season. Unfortunately, the season took a massive hit when Vinny Testaverde ruptured his Achilles Tendon in the first game of the season. Parcells would later put in formerly undrafted free agent Ray Lucas from nearby

Rutgers (whom Parcells had picked up in his New England days and who had followed him to the Jets in 1998) to replace the struggling Rick Mirer - a former 1st round pick of the Seattle Seahawks in 1993 turned journeyman quarterback. Mirer had proven one thing in the NFL. That was that he was not the real deal. Even when he was brought in with the Jets, he wasn't good at all! Now, Mirer is much more focused on co-owning a winery in Napa County, California called Mirror Wine Company. The Jets would go from starting 1-6 to finishing with a 8-8 record and just missing out of the playoffs. This would not only be Parcells arguably best coaching job, but disappointingly be his last with the Jets. He would go on to resign to his role of GM of the Jets. This is where things get got very confusing and, as one might expect, classic Jets.

The Jets, with Parcells recommendation, was to have Belichick take over as the Jets head coach, because technically, Belichick was already the head coach for 2 years. Wait, What!? Yes, you heard me correctly. You see, the Jets have their own, "unique" way of doing things. When Parcels was brought into New York, he was allowed to bring Bill Belichick with him as an assistant. Then a deal was made such that Parcells would be the head coach for a few years, at which point he would retire – as head coach only, because Parcells was also to become General Manager. Then, at that time, Belichick would take over as the head coach. Still with me? Good, because now things get really crazy...

However, at the same time Parcells was ready to retire, the New England Patriots needed a new head coach and owner Robert Kraft wanted Belichick, who had been Parcells assistant in New England. Parcells, who felt he was treated poorly in New England, blocked any communication that the Patriots could have with Belichick. It was announced on January 3rd, 2000 that Bill Belichick was the new Head Coach of the New York Jets, while Parcells would remain GM, as planned. During those 24 hours, Belichick pondered the decision and ultimately he was allowed to speak with the Patriots. He made a very strange decision - one that would haunt the Jets for years to come.

The following day, on January 4th, 2000 the Jets announced an unexpected press conference that involved Belichick. He walked up to the podium with a regular old napkin you get at any supermarket and announced that he was resigning as Jets head coach, effective immediately. HE LASTED ALL OF ONE DAY AND RESIGNED ON

A FREAKING NAPKIN!?!? Yes! Just like that, Belichick was gone, leaving with so many questions and no answers whatsoever.

Three weeks later, Bill Belichick was announced as the new Head Coach of, you guessed it! The New England Patriots.

We all know what happened next. Belichick went on to become possibly the greatest coach in NFL history. As for the Jets? Well they got a nice one year guy in Al "Groan" Groh, who quit after just one season to coach at his alma mater, the University of Virginia.

Groh was succeeded by former player Herm Edwards, a man who had never been a head coach before, but showed promise as an assistant. It was quite ironic, though, that this man, familiar to all denizens of the Meadowlands as the Eagle who took advantage of one of the most inept decisions in NFL history (albeit, luckily, with the co-tenant Giants), would bring ineptitude to a whole new level. Herm Edwards finished with an abysmal 39-41 record in 5 years as the Jets head man. How he stayed on for that long tells you all you need to know about Jets ownership. This man was the master of poor clock management and it showed in the 2004 AFC Divisional Round game vs. Pittsburgh.

The Jets had just intercepted an errant Big Ben Rothlisberger pass and had first and ten on the Pittsburgh 23. At that distance it would pose an opportunity for Doug Brien to slam through a near-chip-shot 37 yard field goal to win the game. On to the AFC Championship!

"The [Steelers fans] were coming up to me," one Jets fan who was at the game told me, "and congratulating me as they filed out of the stands, anticipating the imminent Jets victory. I told 'em, 'Wait! Where are you going? You obviously don't know the Jets!'" Rather than try to move the ball even closer, or even just fall down and keep it where it was, after a Curtis Martin run for no gain, Edwards had his team take TWO knees in a row. So what?

Here's what:

FACT 1: Whenever you take a knee, you lose two yards. So instead of the ball being on the 23, it was now on the 27, meaning that the potentially game winning and "survive and advancing" field goal would have to be a 43 yarder.

FACT 2: NO OPPOSING TEAM HAD EVER MADE A FIELD GOAL LONGER THAN 40 YARDS IN THE HISTORY OF HEINZ FIELD UP TO THAT POINT.

Brien would miss the kick to send the game into

overtime, where the Jets would go on to lose, ironically by a field goal – although one much closer than 43 yards.

Herm Edwards' most famous quote had been, "Hello! You play to win the game"! Even he didn't take his own words to heart. You might think that Jets management might decide right then and there that that was enough. You would be wrong. It took yet another disappointing season before the team, TRADED Edwards to Kansas City in exchange for a 4th round pick... Think about that, a guy with 5 years of ineptitude actually gets traded to a new team! Not fired, not "allowed to resign", not anything face saving, but traded...yeah.

Right after Edwards, The Jets decided to hire a Bill Belichick disciple (I mean, if you can't get the master, maybe...) Eric, "Man-Genius", Mangini. He was the defensive assistant of 3 Super Bowl Champion teams in New England and many believed he would take the Jets to the next level. It looked promising after the Jets went 10-6 in his first year and made the playoffs with NFL comeback Player of the Year, QB Chad Pennington. Things really were going quite well...then it all fell apart – in classic, excruciating Jets fashion.

The following year would begin with some more Bellichick intrigue... After the Jets lost their home opener of 2007, Mangini complained to league officials of the Patriots spying on the Jets plays during the game. This would officially become the infamous "Spygate" affair, which earned Belichick the moniker from Jets fans, "Bill Belicheat".

For the Jets, that would be the high point of the year, as the team finished with a dismal 4-12 record. The Jets would go into 2008 needing a star and they would get that one...5 years too late. The Jets released Chad Pennington and traded for future Hall of Famer Brett Favre. Things really worked out at first for Mangini and Favre. By Thanksgiving many analysts were calling the Jets "the best team in the NFL", as they had started 8-3. But after a huge – and typical - December collapse, which included an embarrassing season ending loss to Pennington and his new Miami team, the rival Miami Dolphins, The Jets would finish 8-8 and miss the playoffs. In fairness, Favre was hurt during that time. But nonetheless Mangini was fired the next day and left a not so pleasant legacy in New York. "Mangenius"? More like "Mandud".

Then we come to the biggest circus of them all. Rex Ryan was hired by the Jets to replace Mangini. Ryan had been late to his interview with the Jets by more than 30 minutes! Ok... Next he actually had gotten a tattoo of his wife in nothing but Mark Sanchez jersey. OK…"Sexy Rexy", as he would come to be known, came with a big presence and an even bigger stomach.   Whatever, this man put the Jets through more turmoil and weird things than any coach before in team history. The man started with so much promise, guiding the Jets, with new franchise QB Mark Sanchez (The Sanchise), to two consecutive AFC Championship appearances.

Along the way came some very odd ordeals. He didn't even realize the team had made the playoffs his first year until someone in the press had to tell him during the post game press conference! Then, in the offseason, he flipped "the bird" at a Dolphins fan in South Florida. After those two incidents, things just got worse and worse. "Sexy Rexy's" tenure was marked with inconsistent play from the offense which included later on, Tim The Savior Tebow, and just poor decision making by himself. But what would you expect from a former long-time defensive coordinator, by nature suspicious and afraid of the offense. This ultimately led the Jets to firing him in 2014.

But did they learn? His successor was YET ANOTHER DEFENSIVE COORDINATOR, one of the most emotion-less and expression-less coaches in Jets history (which, fairly, was a definite change from the volatile Ryan).: Todd Bowles, a man who had never been a head coach before and had limited success as a coordinator. To go from a rah rah, explosive figure to an expression-less, emotion-less leader is something only the Jets could do. Todd Bowles would become, "The Great Stoneface". Why? Because no matter what happened in the game or at his press conference he would have the same facial expression and emotion...LIFELESS! Stone Faced Todd Bowles made Medusa look normal.

It was so bad that in his first year as the Jets coach, he played the last game of the season - mind you, a game the Jets had to win in order to make the playoffs -as just another game. HOW CAN YOU HAVE NO EMOTION OVER THAT! You know who they lost to in that game? The Buffalo Bills and their new head coach...REX RYAN!

If that wasn't bad enough, he was praised for three consecutive 5-11 seasons! THREE YEARS! HOW DO YOU ALLOW THAT TO HAPPEN? He was eventually fired in January of 2019. As for the Jets, they receded to the fringe hell know as "mediocrity"...

7

Not So Free Agents

One of the most intriguing parts of the NFL season is the free agency period. Since 1993, teams, fans, and players always look forward to seeing what big name players go where, in the hope that they can positively impact the teams that choose them. For the Jets and their fans, all they have gotten is many not so free agents. What does that mean you might ask? Well, once you see the deals that were made and the subsequent performance on the field, you, just like many Jets fans, will groan and moan for hours on end.

Another thing worth noting is that the Jets have spent more money on quarterback than any other position. You might ask, well, isn't that true of any franchise? Well, no. You see, the curse of Joe Namath is the real deal my friends. Ever since Super Bowl III, the Jets have struggled to find the next great Jets QB – a so-called "franchise" quarterback - that will lead them back to the promised land. What they get instead is just more heartache and despair. Let's face it, who in their right mind wants to be the quarterback for the New York Jets?

Well, as the old saying goes, "Money talks".

When you think of Franchise Quarterbacks, you think of some of the greats, Joe Montana, Johnny Unitas, Tom Brady. For the Jets, when you think of a Franchise Quarterback, you think of some pretty interesting names. The year was 1993 and the Jets were coming off an abysmal year in which they had gone 4-12 under Bruce Coslet. They also were reeling from very poor play from QB's Browning Nagle and 1983's controversial pick, Ken O'Brien. Neither could get it done and the Jets needed a switch. So, they traded a 3rd round pick to Cincinnati in exchange for Boomer Esiason. A man who just 5 years earlier had led the Bengals to the Super Bowl.

What happened next, would lead us to our first big free agent disaster. Boomer played 3 years for the Jets with 3 different head coaches. He struggled mightily with injuries. This led to him being released by the Jets and forcing them to believe that they had to make a huge splash in free agency. The big name that they went after was someone who nobody expected or understood: Neil O'Donnell.

Neil O'Donnell had just taken the Steelers the previous season to the Super Bowl, only to be smacked around in Super Bowl XXX vs. The Dallas Cowboys 27-17. In that game, O'Donnell threw two questionable interceptions which single handedly lost them the game. Based on that, it was hard to understand precisely what the Jets saw in that game, but they wanted him. He signed prior to the 96 season for an astounding $25,000,000. You heard me right!

Did this signing pay off? O'Donnell went 0-6 to start the season before he was lost for the year due to the first of several injuries. He was not mobile, he seemingly had no awareness, he was paper thin, and Jets teammates questioned his leadership and desire to play because his performance was so counterproductive. He lasted only 2 seasons before Bill Parcels had enough. The team released him prior to the 1998 season. Before his stint with the Jets, O'Donnell had been known as a, "professional" but the only professional thing he showed the Jets was how to make the Jets open their wallets and show him the money!

The next guy wasn't exactly a free agent but a big splash with massive repercussions - none other than the man known as the as the king of the so-called "River Boat Gamblers, Brett Favre.

Yes, the Jets actually at one time had a Hall of Fame QB at the helm...5 years too late. The Jets decided after the 2007 season that they had had enough of the injury prone, Chad Pennington, and released him. What did they do next?

Woody Johnson wanted a big splash and was always looking for that next opportunity for one. So GM Mike Tannenbaum acquired Favre.

The thing was was that Favre never wanted to be a Jet! He wanted to go to the NFC North so he could beat the Packers. But failing to make that happen, he came to New York and the Jets became the talk of the football world. Kersplash!

The Jets and Favre got off to a fast start going 8-3 through 11 weeks. Commentators and pundits anointed them as the best team in the league. Then, after Favre got hurt and started getting a little bit more than friendly with a Jets cheerleader, the Jets faltered and collapsed (December, anyone?) to an 8-8 record, missing out on the playoffs after having gotten eliminated by losing to, of all people, Chad Pennington and the rival Miami Dolphins in the last game of the year.

After the season, Favre left the Jets and moved to the Minnesota Vikings – they of NFC North fame - and took them almost all the way to the Super Bowl the very next year. Ironically, it was an ill-advised classic Brett Favre riverboat gambler interception that ended that run.

Now, at last, we come to possibly one of the biggest publicity stunts that Woody Johnson and the Jets ever made in their history – which is saying a lot, given the string of stunts that had them dominate the "back page" of the NY tabloids. On March 21st, 2012 the Jets traded a 4th and 6th round pick to the Denver Broncos, in exchange for the biggest social media star of that time, Tim Tebow.

Yes, the Jets traded for Tim Tebow. Tebow had just been named the backup in Denver after the Broncos signed Peyton Manning. The Jets saw it as an opportunity to get some competition for Mark Sanchez while Johnson, more importantly, saw it as a chance to get a media star. It was a win-win. The Jets now had two media star qb's in "The Sanchise" and the guy who had invented "Tebowing". It was a match made in Woody Johnson heaven. The only problem was that Tebow...really couldn't play quarterback... AT ALL!

On its face, this could have been a good move. The Jets had just brought in Tony Sparano as offensive coordinator, the famous proponent of the "wildcat formation", a running strategy with which Sparano had had some success while head coach at Miami. But when the trade happened, he and Ryan, while hailing the move, scratched their heads at to how use Tebow, even as Johnson claimed that it had been their idea all along.

In fact, the Jets did use Tebow in the wildcat - but ONLY in wildcat formations and kept using Sanchez in all other quarterback roles instead. It became a point of big controversy when Sanchez was struggling and fans wanted Rex Ryan to bench him for Tebow. But that never happened and Tebow barely saw the field. He lasted only one season in New York, throwing just 8 passes and with 32 rushing attempts. Instead of Tebowing, the Jets should have gotten down and prayed that they wished they hadn't brought him in.

8

The Over The Hill Gang

When you think of building a team, you think of drafting and acquiring young, talented players that can give you sustained success for many years. Especially, when it comes to the quarterback position. However, if you are the Jets, you find every reason on Earth to bring in people who are well past their prime and are looking forward to retiring soon rather than making a Super Bowl run. There is a show out there called, "King of The Hill". Ladies and Gentleman, the Jets are indeed the King...The King of the Over the Hill Gang.

Joe Namath is an icon. There is no question about that. The man single handedly guaranteed that the Jets would win Super Bowl III AND HE DELIVERED! The man was riding on an all time high and it seemed like nothing could stop the man and the Jets. Then, like Joe's knees, everything fell apart. Namath dealt with knee problems since his time at Alabama. The doctors performed surgery on him prior to his rookie year and said he could last at most four years. Well, Namath went much further than four years and in some ways maybe too far.

He would go on to play 12 years with the Jets. Most of the years following the Super Bowl were pretty bad and Namath's injuries were just too much. The Jets made the very bad decision of keeping him around for way too long and giving him way too many chances to come back. This hurt the Jets on the field because after 1970, the Jets would really struggle for the next decade to have success and to find Namath's replacement. This ultimately led the Jets to releasing Namath prior to the 1977 season. He was picked up by the Rams. This one decision – to keep Joe going way beyond when he should have - would be the downfall of Jets QB's for years to come.

The next guy that was a very odd choice was none other than the former Heisman trophy winner, Vinny Testaverde. Testaverde really didn't live up to the hype when he was with the Tampa Bay Bucs. He would become a journeyman quarterback who would have solid years, but nothing that made him a great player. After his time with the Browns and the Ravens, Testaverde became a Jet in 1998 under Bill Parcells, albeit as a backup to then incumbent Glenn Foley. But Foley went down, and then the Jets did the "unthinkable"...THEY MADE TESTAVERDE THE STARTER. But then they RODE HIM ALL THE WAY TO WITHIN ONE WIN FROM

THE SUPER BOWL! Testaverde had his best season as a pro, guiding the Jets to the AFC Championship game vs. the heavily favored Denver Broncos. Even though the Jets would go on to lose that game, there were Super Bowl aspirations for the Jets heading into the 1999 season.

You know where I'm going with this, Jets fans. Late in the first half, of the first game of the season, Testaverde blew out his achilles and the Jets dreams were dashed...AGAIN!!! The Jets were actually lucky to go 8-8 that year, with the help of unheralded former Rutgers star Ray Lucas, but by the time they landed upon him they had dug themselves too deep a hole with the disappointing Rick Mirer, and missed the playoffs.

Unfortunately for Jets fans and Testaverde, things never got better. Testaverde struggled with injuries, despite guiding the Jets to the postseason in 2001. He would eventually be replaced by Chad Pennington and stayed on the Jets for far too long. This was just another chapter of how being a Jets fan gets old.

Then, we come to two guys who personified the 21st century so far - not just the Over the Hill Gang, but The WAY Over the Hill Gang. Prior to the 2015/16 season, The Jets needed a new QB after underachiever Geno Smith broke his jaw in a locker room fight with a teammate. (Yeah, that really happened). The Jets needed a man who had experience, somebody who was going to be a leader on and off the field, somebody with an impressive background, somebody who was ready to lead the Jets to glory! Someone like... Ryan Fitzpatrick??.

YUP! Fitzmagic was traded to the Jets from the Texans for a late-round conditional pick. That is how much worth he actually had.

Fitzpatrick had come from prestigious Harvard (a college known far more for academics than athletic prowess) and had scored a 48 out of 50 on the Wonderlic test for NFL prospects accordingly. Unfortunately, this didn't translate to success on the field. Not even close.

For the entirety of his 10 year (10!!!) journeyman career, he had been mediocre at best - for the Rams, Bengals, Bills, Titans, and most recently the Texans. No matter – somehow, the Jets saw Fitzpatrick as the guy with the proven track record. Well he certainly had a proven track record, just not the one Jets fans were hoping for.

What happened next would just be another, "wonderful", period in Jets history. There was still some "Fitzmagic" left in Ryan as he had his best season as a pro with 3,905 yards passing and an impressive 31 touchdowns. But was that just the Second Coming of the Testaverde Miracle, that would end the same way?

The Jets stood on the brink of the postseason heading into the final game of the 2014 season against Sexy Rexy Ryan and the Bills in week 17. It was then that the clock struck twelve on the miracle season and "Fitzmagic" turned into "Fitzception". He proceeded to throw two bad interceptions at the end of the game as the Jets were driving for the winning score. The Jets would lose and miss out on the playoffs for the fifth year in a row. It would have been bad enough if the saga ended there. But then came the offseason.

Fitzpatrick was a free agent after the 2015 year and he demanded money, A LOT OF MONEY! He actually wanted $18 million from the Jets. The Jets proceeded to laugh him out of the building, as they should have. After all it HAD been a miracle, it had been "magic". To expect another miracle season from a senior citizen with a dubious track record was too much to ask.

But then the Jets realized a month or so later that they didn't have anyone better than him. They decided to give him a 1 year, $12 million guaranteed contract. EVEN THOUGH NOBODY ELSE IN THE LEAGUE EVEN GAVE HIM AN OFFER! That should have been the red

flag right there, but this is the Jets, red flags be damned!
We are going to the Bowl! Perhaps they were referring to
the Toilet Bowl...?

The Jets reverted back to dirt as they went a pathetic 5-
11. After such a forgettable season they had finally seen
enough of the magic that was Fitz and voided his contract.
Would the Jets recover from this mistake and rebound?
Come on Jets fans, you know where this goes right?

After that travesty, the Jets decided to go even older at
the QB position and signed Josh McCown. Why?
Because he , too, represented "experience". McCown was
the ultimate journey quarterback, even more so than the
creaky Fitzpatrick, having already played for 9 teams
BEFORE he ever got to the Jets. I am not making that up!
The man had played for nearly a third of the the NFL
before joining the Jets, HIS 10TH DIFFERENT TEAM!
He would become the ultimate mediocre Jets quarterback.
He posted a 5-8 record as the starter and never got going.

The following year, the Jets finally traded up to draft
USC standout Sam Darnold with the 3rd overall selection
in the 2018 NFL Draft – a chance for a young franchise
quarterback. McCown would lose the starting job to
Darnold and did not play the entire 2018 season,
becoming instead a mentor to young Darnold.

The Jets loved quarterbacks with time-worn reputations. The only issue was that they were much more time-worn than reputation, and were all on the other side of their careers. It also leads into one of the biggest parts of being a suffering Jets fan, dealing with ownership.

9

Who Runs This Team, Anyway!?!?

When you are a fan of any team in any sport, you want your owner to care, not just about making money, but also about putting the team in the best position to succeed and be great on the field. There are many owners out there that are like that, Robert Kraft of the NFL's New England Patriots, Joe Lacob and Peter Guber of the NBA's Golden State Warriors, and even Mario Lemieux of the NHL's Pittsburgh Penguins. Those are the type of owners you want.

Jets fans have none of that. In fact they have everything backwards in their world. You want to talk about where all the problems I've mentioned usually start? They originate with ownership.

The first owner of the Jets was a man by the name of David Abraham "Sonny" Werblin. He bought the Titans of New York of the American Football League in 1963 from Harry Wismer. Once purchased, Werblin renamed and rebranded the team into the Jets because they were going to play in Shea Stadium, the home of the New York

Mets, as well as the fact that the stadium was right next to LaGuardia Airport. Werblin was also a very famous talent agent for some of the biggest names in TV and Film, such as Jackie Gleason and Marilyn Monroe.

So Werblin was all about show business and he wanted a star for his team. He got that star when he drafted and then signed Joe Namath to a record $400,000 deal. Sonny was the man that built the Jets into not just an entertaining team, but a talented team. So much so, that the Jets went all the way and won Super Bowl III in what is considered by many to be the greatest game ever played. He put the Jets on the map and made them the most marketable team in professional football at the time.

Unfortunately, the ride would end sooner than expected. Leon Hess became part owner of the team with Sonny Werblin in 1963. Hess was a self-made man from Asbury Park, New Jersey who struck gold in the oil business. He would later go on to buy out Werblin in 1968 to become the full owner of the Jets. During Hess ownership, he went through the trials and tribulations that came with many failed coaching and player hires. He just continued to make what proved to be bad hire after bad hire and the Jets continued to struggle and fall into unabated mediocrity.

The biggest move he ever made was in 1984, when he moved the Jets out of their long time home, Shea Stadium, and across the Hudson to share Giants Stadium with their ("big") brother franchise, the New York Giants.

Hess was a good man, but bad decisions ultimately hurt the team in the long run. He tried to do his best for the fans. But even when he made great moves – like hiring Parcells and the heir apparent Belichick, they backfired. Some Jets fans wanted Hess out 20 years prior to his selling the team. Eventually they got their wish.

The next man to own the Jets needs no introduction – even as now he is making introductions in Great Britain as US Ambassador. I am of course talking about Woody Johnson, of the famous Johnson & Johnson fortune. This family has personified the pain of being a fan of the organization.

Woody bought the team in 2000 from Hess for an astounding $635 million. He outbid what some call the worse owner in sports, none other than James Dolan of the New York Knicks. Can you imagine, Jets fans? James Dolan nearly owned the Jets! Those Knicks fans who are also Jets fans might have passed out at the thought of that!

The sale came on the heels of nearly getting a deal done to build a new stadium for the Jets - in the heart of

Manhattan, no less! To hear Buffalo Bills fans tell it, theirs is the only team playing in New York. Obviously, such a bold move as playing in the Big Apple itself would put an end to such silly claims. But, of course, like everything else, the Jets failed to get this done and stayed at Giants Stadium.

It was somewhat embarrassing for the team to play in a stadium named after another team, an embarrassment that many Jets fans did not take well. To his credit though, Johnson partnered with the Giants to get Metlife stadium built, so it's not as bad as it may sound. But this was only the tip of the iceberg for what Johnson was going to do. (Iceberg... Where have I heard that before? The Jets started out as the Titans... You know, as in The Titanic...)

Johnson was the architect behind the hirings of Rex Ryan and stone-faced Todd Bowles. This owner clearly wanted to have guys who had personalities! Even if the personality had no personality (cf, Bowles). Why you might ask? Well, because there is no such thing as bad publicity and Johnson wanted the Jets to be the most talked about team in New York City, day in and day out. Well, he got his wish, but for many bad reasons.

From Brett Favre texting nudes (or at least nude parts..) to a Jets employee, to Rex Ryan having a tattoo of his wife in nothing but a Sanchez jersey, Woody Johnson made millions from the exposure, setting the stage for the infamous PSL's that Jets fans were forced to pay in order just to purchase season tickets. Remember, this man hired Rex Ryan even after Ryan was 45 minutes late to his interview for the head coaching job! Why?

Who knows? But whatever, he wound up spending money not on winning but instead on dominating the back pages of tabloid newspapers with blaring headlines, good or bad. Usually bad. Not about how well the team was doing on the field and in the standings.

The first move was when Woody was able to get the Jets on HBO's, "Hard Knocks". The team was coming off a deep playoff run from the previous year in which they fell a little short to the Indianapolis Colts in the AFC Championship. So HBO gave the fans the behind the scenes look at the team preparing for the 2010 season. "Hard Knocks" presented a lot; from Rex Ryan's snack raid, to Darelle Revis' contract holdout, to even Jets players eating cheeseburgers during practice at Hofstra. What the show did is reveal the circus behind a Rex Ryan led training camp. But remember – everyone loves the circus! The Jets became the talk of the NFL, whether in a good or bad light.

Then Rex Ryan decided to flip the bird to a fan. Even before "Hard Knocks", Ryan was doing a ringside interview with a Showtime reporter in Miami. Since the interview could be heard throughout the arena, every Dolphins fan could hear what Ryan had to say. He made a bold prediction through a chorus of boos, "I just want to tell everyone in Miami that we're coming to beat you twice next year." As Rex was leaving the arena, he proceeded to flash his middle finger to some fans with a huge smirk on his face. This made Ryan a hero among Jets fans and the talk of the New York sports media. He was later fined for his actions and was forced to apologize for what he did. But the Jets once again dominated the back pages.

If "The Bird" sent shock waves throughout the tri-state area, the next misadventure really shook it up. This story takes place in early September of 2010. Mexico's TV Azteca sportscaster Ines Sainz was at a practice working on a story on Quarterback Mark Sanchez. While she was there she had footballs thrown at her by a Jets coach, players on the team saw fit to hurl cat-calls while she was in the team's locker room. This led to a whole investigation of the team and Woody Johnson himself. Eventually this embarrassing kerfuffle was resolved with a statement of apology from the Jets organization. But perhaps more importantly there was a lot of publicity - backlash, mostly, but publicity nonetheless. Say what you will, it did give the Jets what the ownership craved - much more coverage.

But the hits just kept on coming! The next stunt really packed a punch. During the 2015 preseason, there was a fight between quarterback Geno Smith and linebacker IK Enemkpali. At one point Geno was punched directly in the face and ended up with a broken jaw. The reason for this scuffle? Money: $600 to be exact. The story goes, Enemkpali paid for Geno's plane ticket to attend his July 11 football camp at Pflugerville High School in Texas. However, days before the camp, a person close to Smith was killed in a motorcycle accident in Miami and Smith did not attend Enemkpali's camp, according to sources.

Since Geno did not attend the camp, IK demanded Geno pay back the money that IK had spent on his plane ticket. Smith told him that he would pay him back, but he never actually did. This led to Enemkpali confronting Geno in the locker and then the two went at it. The fight, or more importantly, the starter's broken jaw, became a huge topic of discussion for several weeks in New York and the entire football world. The result? An even brighter spotlight on the Jets than they would get for their play on the field that season.

But out of all the stories we have just mentioned, none is more of a perfect example of what Woody Johnson wanted, publicity-wise, than the saga of Brett Favre. The Jets acquired him via a trade after Favre decided to come out of retirement. The Packers didn't want him around anymore and thus shipped him to the last place he wanted to go. Favre wanted to go to the Vikings, but instead ended up with Gang Green.

Favre played well the first half of the season, leading the team to an 8-3 record and garnering buzz about the Jets being the "best team in the NFL", but, due to injuries, his play fell off after Thanksgiving and the Jets missed the postseason in Favre's only season in the Big Apple – yet another Jets December swoon.

But even with all that, the biggest story on Favre that season was again something off the field that was headline-grabbing. Brett Favre was considered a gunslinger on the field. But nobody ever mentioned the possibility that he was one off the field as well. This story is strange and unreal, but also just too hilarious not to mention.

While he was with the Jets, Favre began flirting with

Jenn Sterger who, at the time, was a TV personality with the Jets. He allegedly texted certain pictures, pictures of his junk, to Sterger's cell phone. He also left her several voicemails. He tried to get in contact with her through Myspace (feel old yet?), using another Jet employee to try to get into contact with her. You might imagine that this, um, exposure would result in shame and disaster. You would be wrong. There were instead headlines all over the country – not just on the back pages of New York tabloids - which shed quite a different light on the reputation of the future Hall of Fame Quarterback – but more importantly, a great deal of coverage, albeit dubious, of the Jets as well.

What do all these misadventures have in common? Publicity. And again, there is no such thing as bad publicity...

What other made-for-publicity moves did Johnson make? Well, how about bringing in Tim Tebow? As a fan you might go, "WHY THE HELL WOULD WE BRING HIM IN! HE CAN'T EVEN THROW A FOOTBALL! WHAT IS WRONG WITH THESE PEOPLE???"

Again, one word - publicity. It was another move to make headlines and grab the spotlight in the New York media. Oh, and perhaps, just perhaps, make inroads with Tebow's rather "devoted" following...?

Johnson claimed it wasn't his idea to bring Tebow in; he did it at the prompting of the coaching staff. But then why were Ryan and offensive coordinator Tony Sparano – the biggest proponent of the "wildcat" offense, seemingly tailor-made for a running QB like Tebow – scratching their heads when Tebow came aboard as to what to do with him...?

While the Giants were winning championships during that period, it was the Jets who were making headlines 24/7 because of all these ridiculous moves. Look at all the coaches and players Johnson has brought in during his tenure and that speaks for itself. But it only gets worse from here ladies and gentlemen. Why, you may ask?

Well, in 2017, Woody took the job of being President Donald Trump's Ambassador to the United Kingdom. Thus he would need someone to take over the team. Whoever might THAT be? Why, none other than his brother Chris Johnson, of course! Chris, just like Woody, made moves that were based on keeping the public eye on the Jets, whether they were good, bad, or indifferent. He let Todd Bowles last two more years of 5-11 than he should have, by all rights. He also let Mike Maccagnan stay on as GM, even though Maccagnan was continuing to prove that he wasn't getting the job done. (It should be noted that Bowles avoided being fired because, although the Jets went 5-11 in 2017, the team was projected to go 2-14! So relatively, the season had been a success!)

Chris finally fired Todd Bowles after the 2018 season, topping consecutive 5-11 campaigns with an even more abysmal 4-12 one. He oddly kept Maccagnan on as GM and together they began to search for a new Head Coach. And just whom did they hire? Was it a big name like Mike McCarthy, who actually wanted to come to New York, or an up and coming college coach in Lincoln Riley? Nope! They hired wide eyes Adam Gase, the former head coach of the Miami Dolphins, WHO MIAMI HAD JUST FIRED A FEW WEEKS PREVIOUSLY AFTER A SUB-MEDIOCRE LOSING SEASON! ARE YOU FREAKING KIDDING ME? Undeterred, the Jets hired Gase and hoped he could expedite the development of franchise QB Sam Darnold and the offense. This was a move that made very little sense (of course) to Jets fans and the media.

Then, in early May of 2019 reports surfaced about a rift between Gase and Maccagnan, particularly about how to spend money on free agents. This came out well after the Jets had signed big name free agent, running back Le'Veon Bell. It was also reported that Gase didn't like or want Bell in the first place. Gase came out on May 9th in a press conference to say that those reports were false and it "pisses me off" that people were saying that.

Well, he might have been saying that tongue-in-cheek. A week later on May 16th, Chris Johnson announced that Maccagnan and Vice President Brian Heimerdinger were fired. This was the atom bomb Jets fans were waiting for! Maccagnan's replacement? Adam Gase. Hmmm, doesn't that seem odd that the reports that had initially come out as false actually turned out to be true? Only the Jets...

Johnson came out and even stated that he wasn't really looking for someone experienced to be the new GM. Two names came up - Daniel Jeremiah from NFL Network and Peyton Manning. Wait, what? PEYTON MANNING?? Incredibly, the Jets were looking at either a draft analyst with no relevant experience in the front office, or a QB (albeit a Hall of Famer) also with no GM experience. Sure! Why not? You can't make this up!

Chris Johnson had actually outdone his brother!! The team, as of this writing is still without a GM. Who will it be? Your guess is as good as mine.

10

Stop! They're Already Dead!

There's an old saying: Stop beating the dead horse. All right, already – I get it, I understand your point! No need to pile on!

Jets fans not only suffer watching this team on the field, but also with a) Where their money is going, b) How much money they are forced to pay, and c) Is their home field really theirs? This organization hits you any way possible and forces you to do things that hurt you physically, financially and emotionally. The Jets are among the leading teams doing this, not just in football, but in all of sports.

We've spent an entire chapter about the money that has been wasted on players, from draft busts like Vernon Gholston to used-to-be-greats like Brett Favre to over the hill players that nobody else wanted but that didn't keep the Jets from overpaying, like Ryan Fitzpatrick. It makes you wonder – why are they spending all that money for so little return?

In fact, you couldn't blame Jets fans for wondering, sometimes out loud, sometimes VERY LOUDLY,

"Where is the team getting all that money to blow to begin with...?"

When you think of Jets fans, you might ask where they all live and where they are from. There are clearly many Jets fans in New Jersey and in New York City. However, a huge chunk of fans of the team are on Long Island, where the Jets were when they experienced their brief glory days, and in the Long Island suburbs. Unfortunately for those fans, they have to make the long trek to the Meadowlands to see their team. The Meadowlands – the NEW JERSEY Meadowlands, home of... GIANTS STADIUM. What about building a new stadium on the Island and moving there? You would kill two birds with one stone – a new home all their own much closer to the traditional fan base! Some say it makes way too much sense and the Jets don't do things that make sense. Far better, their thinking goes, to just force their fans to spend money on gas, tolls, and tickets (to say nothing of the attendant aggravation!) just to get to the stadium for a game. To watch their team year after year underperform and flirt with disaster. Yeah, that's the ticket!

And speaking of tickets...

In 2005, Woody Johnson was in the works with New York City to move the Jets from the Meadowlands to

midtown Manhattan. Sure, it wasn't Long Island, but it
was a lot closer than the Meadowlands, and it was a lot
better to think of the team playing in the Big Apple than in
a big "swamp". For once, the Jets would stand out in the
NFL! In fact, the whole New York Metropolitan sports
world in general! How amazing would that have been!?
And think of the draw, the prestige, the allure it would
have given the Jets in attracting top notch players and
coaches!

Jets fans, you might want to stop reading at this point
because you know where this goes.

The stadium plan was eventually dismissed. It was
rejected by the Metropolitan Transit Authority,
responsible for running the subways and buses that would
service the site. The location for the stadium was
proposed to be where the former New York Central rail
yards had been, which was on the west side of Manhattan.
City officials worried that parking and traffic control in
the area would have been an absolute disaster, given that
many fans like to tailgate and have the full fan experience.
In the middle of the biggest city in the country, that
experience would not be easy to accommodate. Even
former New York City mayor Rudy Giuliani, a proven
booster of such projects as the new Yankee Stadium and

Citi Field, was against the idea of a stadium on the West Side and called for immediate rejection of the plan.

The situation was made even more complex by the fact that this area was partially owned by one Donald J. Trump, and thus it should come as no surprise that part of said area was slated for more high rise apartment buildings. The proposed stadium, on top of any new residential development, was deemed by the MTA to be too much of a financial burden and thus the MTA rejected it. And with that rejection, the funding commitment from the City, so critical for such an ambitious project, dried up.

Other locations in the City, including Flushing, the location of Shea Stadium, the home of the team in the Namath years, were proposed. However, the Jets and Woody Johnson did not want to move to anywhere other than the West Side. They said that any place other than there was worse than staying in New Jersey.

And so, on June 6th 2005, New York State Assembly Speaker Sheldon Silver, New York State Senate Majority Leader Joseph Bruno, and Governor George Pataki all abstained in the vote to build the stadium, and thus did the Jets' dream crash.

Thus did politics interfere with the Jets obtaining

satisfaction. But even in such failure, it is to be remembered that there is no such thing as bad publicity. What would have happened if the stadium had been built? All the Jets and their fans can do is sit around and dream. Just like everything else...

The Jets instead wound up staying in that big "swamp", known as the Meadowlands. They did partner with the Giants to build a new, state of the art (but mysteriously un-domed) stadium, Metlife Stadium. Despite that fact, the Jets are still seen as second class citizens to the Giants.

And what did the new stadium bring? A new era of success? A Super Bowl title? After all, many teams inaugurate their new stadiums with championships. Would the Jets be among them?

Why, no, of course. What the new stadium brought Jets fans were - The dreaded PSL's. What are PSLs? PSL stands for "Personal Seat License", which entitles the holder to buy season tickets for a certain seat in a stadium. At an additional cost, of course... An additional cost that far exceeds the price of the season tickets the holder of the PSL is trying to buy. By a lot.

True, the holder can sell the seat license to someone else if they no longer wish to purchase season tickets. The only catch is that the owner of the venue has the right to change the price of those tickets to whatever they please, whenever they please. There is your lesson for the day – a lesson Jets fans have learned oh so well.

For Jets fans, this part of the process has done nothing but make people question about life decisions and why they are Jets fans in the first place.

And of course, ticket prices have gone up year in and year out, irrespective of whether the team has improved or not. This has forced many long time Jets fans to give up their season tickets. We are talking about fans who have seen this hot mess of a team for 20+ years and now have decided to give it all away. They simply can't take it any more!

It got so bad that in early 2018, a fan actually sued the team and MetLife Stadium because HE had to pay the PSL while some other fans did NOT. Unfortunately, this fan wasn't the only one who got the short end of the stick. There were other fans who had to pay EVEN MORE! That's how bad it got for some Jets fans - the money they had to spend on this team was way too much, ESPECIALLY GIVEN HOW MASSIVELY POOR THE PRODUCT ON THE FIELD WAS!

Jets fans will tell you - THIS TEAM MAKES

PEOPLE WORRY ABOUT THEIR FINANCIAL STABILITY AS WELL AS THEIR OWN PSYCHOLOGICAL WELL BEING! JETS FANS FEEL THAT THIS TEAM DOES NOTHING, BUT MAKE YOU GO BROKE, WITHOUT ANY GLIMMER OF HOPE THAT THINGS WILL GET BETTER! THEY RIP YOU OFF AT THE BOX OFFICE, THEY RIP YOU OFF WITH OWNERSHIP AND TEAM BUILDING, AND MOST IMPORTANTLY, THEY RIP YOU OFF ON THE FIELD, YEAR AFTER YEAR AFTER YEAR! YOU CAN'T MAKE THIS STUFF UP!

It doesn't get any worse than being a Jets fan, they will tell you! The fans feel the Jets should be paying them, not the other way around.   Fans get killed by the prices, they get killed by all the bad moves, and they especially get killed every time the team takes the field.

So before you kill the Jets in front of their fans, just remember – they've been through a lot, they're going through a lot and, unless things drastically change soon, they will be going through a lot for the foreseeable future. In other words, stop beating them.

THEY'RE ALREADY DEAD!

11

It Wasn't Always This Way...

I have spent a LOT of time revisiting every heartbreak, every heartache, every depressing, agonizing, ironic, excruciating thing that has happened to the Jets and their fans. It feels like this team has never had any good memories or times. It seems like we can't find one time - just one! - when things were happy and peaceful.

However, there were and have been times when it actually was this way. There were times when the Jets were praised by commentators, their fans and the NFL in general. There were people who brought great memories for fans to cherish for years.

In the 60's and into the 70's the Jets were one of the most successful and most envied franchises in sports, thanks to one man and one man's vision only: Mr. Sonny Werblin. This man gave the Jets tools to succeed and it paid off in spades. He drafted Joe Namath, paid him like crazy and made the Jets the most glamorous team in football. He brought his team to Monmouth Park in Oceanport, New Jersey, for training camp, thereby expanding the base of Jets fans beyond Long Island and

New York City. You had a man who tried anything and everything to get the Jets a championship and make them millions of dollars. The thing is, he actually did it!

You had a coach in Weeb Ewbank who came from the mighty Baltimore Colts of the NFL, where he had led them to multiple championships, and turned the Jets into a dominant franchise that upset those same Colts in Super Bowl III. You had a coach who made Joe Namath into one of the greatest passers in football history. His coaching made Namath the first QB to throw for over 4000 yards in a season, turning him into the legend he would become - a Hall of Famer.

Then you have that man himself, Mr. Broadway Joe Willy Namath. He was a man from Beaver Falls, Pennsylvania, out of the University of Alabama, who came in with his long flowing hair and white shoes and dazzled many fans and opponents for years on the fields of Shea Stadium and throughout the NFL. He was a quarterback who broke records with the flick of his wrist, seemingly with no effort at all. Namath was a man who not only predicted a win, but guaranteed that the Jets would beat the Colts in the Super Bowl, AND DELIVERED ON IT! This man made the Jets the most talked about team in football for decades.

You see Jets fans, it wasn't always bad, you don't always have to want to shoot yourself or wonder why the football gods above made you Jets fans. What did you ever do to gain such disfavor?? You can look at that time period and even the time period of Bill Parcells and say to yourself, "You know, if it happened before, it can happen again".

Just remember one thing, when other fans ask you how could the team trade this guy or sign that guy, or how can they hire such an incompetent person to run the team or have an owner who is learning on the job, all you have to do is look them in the eyes, smile and say these three words:

"Only the Jets…"

EPILOGUE
...But That Was Then; This is Now

It's September 8th 2019. A new season. A new regime. A young quarterback that portends to really be the franchise QB who would lead them on to former glory. A new hope (cue the Star Wars intro).

The Jets are playing their division rival Buffalo Bills at home. And they are dominating. They dominate in the first quarter. They dominate at halftime. And at the end of the third quarter the Jets have a dominating 16-3 lead. The Bills look lifeless, defeated, dominated...

Tell me - Did the Jets complete the victory in dominating fashion? Did the Jets eek out a well deserved victory? Did the Jets even let go of the rope and get defeated in a blowout?

No. When all the styrene butadiene ("crumb rubber") has settled, the final score: Jets 16, Buffalo 17.

Yes, Jets fans, yet another ironic, agonizing, excruciating loss.

Just.

Enough.

To.

Succumb…

But wait! There's more!

Just four days later, as the Jets were trying to recoup from that Jets-like loss and pull it together for the rest of the still young season, they announce that Le'Veon Bell is hurt. How long will the biggest offseason acquisition and key part of the Jets hope for the offense be out?

Before that question can even begin to be answered (it subsequently turned out that he would not lose any serious time), another bombshell: MONO. As in mononucleosis. "The Kissing Disease". The Jets have learned that Sam Darnold, the new savior, has Mono. Has the team just kissed the season goodbye?

How long will HE be out? A week? A couple of weeks? Till November? The problem is, no one knows. Mono is an insidious disease. It's not easy to accurately predict how long it will take for a full recovery.

Thus the Jets are in a tantalizing netherworld. They can't expect to get him back quickly; they can't rule him out for the season. All they know is Mono can cause the spleen to become enlarged and rupture, especially as a result of contact. If they bring him back too soon, he could die. So, like 1999, 2003, 2015, the Jets will have to

endure the next several games with a backup at
quarterback.

September 16, 2019. It's Monday night! The Jets go
into the game being led by backup QB Trevor Siemian - a
man with multiple years of experience as the starting
quarterback of an NFL team. Thus, they should be in
good hands until Darnold has finished nursing his illness.
It's not optimal, but at least they will be led by a seasoned
NFL starter - caliber field general.

But, in the middle of the second quarter, Siemian goes
down with an injury. This time, there is no uncertainty.
Siemian is out for the season.

Taxi! In comes the quarterback of the practice squad,
Luke Faulk. The Cleveland Browns look like THEY'RE
having an open practice as they walk away with a 20 point
margin of victory. The Jets, led by a QB clearly
overmatched by the moment, go on a mini - road trip of
two games during which they are embarrassed both times.
Then they would return home to face the playoff
contending Dallas Cowboys.

Will they be embarrassed again? Would it be another
blowout? Will the Jets fans be muttering, "Just, End, The,
Season"?

Are you kidding!?!? This is the Jets!!! Tantalizing

doesn't just happen on the down side - it happens on the upside as well! Sam Darnold announces during the week that he has been cleared by the doctors and the Jets medical staff to return as the starter for Game 5!

And so what do the Jets do? THEY DOMINATE! Although the final score has them winning by only two points, the game was not as close as the score. J-E-T-S JETS, JETS, JETS!

This is what it's like to be a Jets fan: Your hopes and dreams go sky high into the Jet stream, only to have them immediately dashed in ironic, agonizing, excruciating fashion. And then, just when you think all is lost, they stage a miraculous victory that keeps you on the hook.

That is the state of the Jets at the time of this writing. You, dear friend, by the time you are reading this, probably already know how the rest of the season plays out. Will they have returned to their losing ways? Will they have run the table and made the playoffs? Will they have continued that great tradition of Jets mediocrity...?

One thing is certain: However it all plays out, it will happen in a way that can be done by...

Only the Jets...

Made in the USA
Middletown, DE
16 February 2020

84754341R00078

J – E – T - S!

PAIN! PAIN!

PAIN!

The Agony and the Ecstasy

(Nah, no ecstasy!)

of the Jets Fan

Neil Villapiano

Nosebleeds Books

ISBN: 978-0-578-63907-9

Copyright © 2019 Neil Villapiano.
All rights reserved.
No part of this book may be reproduced or transmitted in
any form or by any means, electronic or mechanical,
including photocopying, recording, or by any information
storage and retrieval system, without prior permission in
writing from the Author.

Villapiano, Neil
J-E-T-S Pain! Pain! Pain!/ Neil Villapiano. —1st ed. p.
cm.

Printed and Manufactured in the United States of America

Also available as an eBook